MILES MINOR KELLOGG

and the

ENCINITAS BOATHOUSES

MILES MINOR KELLOGG

— *and the* —

ENCINITAS BOATHOUSES

Rachel Brupbacher

RACHEL BRUPBACHER

THE
History
PRESS

Published by The History Press
Charleston, SC
www.historypress.com

Copyright © 2021 by Rachel Brupbacher
All rights reserved

Front cover: Color photo of the Boathouses. *Courtesy of the Encinitas Historical Society.*
Back cover: Portrait of Miles Minor Kellogg. *Author's collection.*

First published 2021

Manufactured in the United States

ISBN 9781467149303

Library of Congress Control Number: 2021934133

To My Grandmother
Betty McWhinny Aldrich (1925–1997)

Her full nature…spent itself in channels which had no great name on the earth.
But the effect of her being on those around her was incalculably diffusive: for
the growing good of the world is partly dependent on unhistoric acts; and that
things are not so ill with you and me as they might have been, is half owing to the
number who lived faithfully a hidden life, and rest in unvisited tombs.

—George Eliot, from Middlemarch

Lives of great men all remind us
We can make our lives sublime,
And, departing, leave behind us
Footprints on the sands of time.

Footprints, that perhaps another,
Sailing o'er life's solemn main,
A forlorn and shipwrecked brother,
Seeing, shall take heart again.

Let us then be up and doing,
With a heart for any fate;
Still achieving, still pursuing,
Learn to labor and to wait.

—*Longfellow, from "A Psalm of Life"*

CONTENTS

ACKNOWLEDGEMENTS

D ue to the remarkable completeness of the Kellogg family archive, I was fortunate to be able to draw the vast majority of my information for this book from private and primary sources, including but not limited to memoirs, oral histories, personal papers and photographs. For the sake of the reader's convenience, I have dispensed with annotating information that was derived from sources not readily available to the public, except in the case of direct quotations. For the sake of consistency as well as readability, I have also taken the liberty of adjusting the grammar, punctuation and spelling in certain pieces of this unpublished material. Such editing applies in particular to the handwritten papers of Miles Minor Kellogg and his brother Porter.

Nevertheless, no book is written in a vacuum, and I am indebted to not a few individuals and organizations that assisted me in my research. Since Ruth Kellogg and her children tended to be elderly men and women when they recorded their memories, certain inaccuracies inevitably surfaced in the stories they left behind. Many of these errors I was able to rectify (and much of the remaining information I was able to crosscheck) by consulting various historical societies, libraries, newspaper archives and senior members of the present-day Kellogg family.

Among those to whom I owe thanks are the following: Marti Anderson and Wendy Hall, archivist and branch manager, respectively, of the Carnegie Library for Local History in Boulder, Colorado, for trying to help me locate some of the houses that Miles built in Boulder; Lois Aufmann, docent of the Encinitas Historical Society, for providing me with recent information about Miles's log cabin in Leucadia; Carolyn Cope, president of the Encinitas Historical Society, for giving me permission to use the society's images of the Boathouses and the Hammond Hotel; Katharine Van Arsdale and Vivian Geow, Special Collections librarian and Academic Records specialist, respectively, at Pacific Union College (PUC) for helping me establish or confirm the Kellogg children's dates and courses of study at PUC; Dr. George Gibson, former professor of history and economics at Union College (Lincoln, Nebraska), for reviewing my information about the history of the American West; and Holly Bauer of the Burns Branch Library and Ron Burkett of Burns Insurance in Burns, Wyoming, for helping me locate the present site of the "little Kellogg schoolhouse," which, even after the passage of more than a century, still braves the whipping winds where it stands on the Wyoming prairies.

Of even greater value was the assistance that I received from numerous members of the present-day Kellogg family. These relatives generously contributed to the completion of this book by sharing their own memories, photographs and genealogical research or (just as importantly) by offering their encouragement. In particular, I would like to thank Winona Kellogg Aastrup; Cindy Kellogg Chesbro and her husband, Wesley; Miles James "Jim" Kellogg and his wife, Laverne; William Lloyd "Bill" Kellogg; Cheryl Brown Maas; Dorothy Kellogg Rice; Rochelle St. Pierre Smith; Evangeline McWhinny St. Pierre; Lamont St. Pierre; Karen Kellogg Stephen; Eloise Kellogg Thomas; and Kathleen Priebe Tonn-Oliver.

Above all, I am indebted to my grandmother the late Betty McWhinny Aldrich and my mother, Nancy Aldrich Brupbacher. For many years the chief family archivist and historian, my grandmother conducted most of the research that made this book possible. It was she who took the trouble of recording oral histories with her many aunts and uncles and transcribing her telephone conversations with them. It was she who, in her quest to evoke the clearest possible picture of the family history, contacted far-flung relatives and traveled to various sites of family significance throughout North America, often with her elderly mother, Edith, in tow and always with a camera in hand. Moreover, as one of only two of Miles Minor Kellogg's grandchildren to have lived with him both in Encinitas and Potrero, she further added to the fund of family knowledge by documenting her own reminiscences of life in his household. Following her death in 1997, this irreplaceable archive lay forgotten in my grandfather's house for nearly twenty years. It was due entirely to my mother's tenacity and (often literally) painstaking efforts that it was saved from destruction after my grandfather's death in 2014. Without the efforts of these two women, much or most of Miles Minor Kellogg's story would have been lost forever, and this book could never have been written.

As a final note of thanks, I would like to express my heartfelt gratitude to all those friends and relatives who sustained the writing of this book by offering words of encouragement when doubts beset me, my energy waned or my spirits flagged. Thank you to all who have so kindly lent such support.

INTRODUCTION

On a fall afternoon in 1929, a slope-shouldered, gray-mustachioed man puttered between two large boats. He had brainstormed for over a year, designing the vessels carefully in his mind before bringing them into reality that October. Now he was adding some finishing touches—anchors carved from redwood.

As he stepped back to survey his work, he could hear the muffled roar of the surf from the Pacific Ocean as the breakers swept over the shore beneath the cliffs a few blocks away. The bright Southern California sunlight flashed against the lenses of his horn-rimmed spectacles, temporarily blinding him. When the glare faded, he eyed the boats critically. Both of them approximately fifty-nine feet long, twenty-one feet tall and lined on each side with portholes, they mirrored each other almost perfectly from their "moorings" on a rise facing away from the ocean.

The man, Miles Minor Kellogg, appeared pleased with his work.

He was not the only one who was impressed. Boats were hardly a rare sight in the sleepy little coastal town of Encinitas, but this pair had attracted an inordinate amount of attention from the start.

One reason for this was the reputation of their creator. Miles was a well-known local figure. Since his arrival in Encinitas over a decade earlier, he had made a name for himself as the owner of Kellogg & Son, a thriving construction company that was responsible for erecting many, if not most, of the houses that emerged throughout Encinitas during the town's 1920s building boom. He was further distinguished by his thrifty ways, to the point that posterity would dub him Encinitas's "ultimate recycler." The material for the two boats was a case in point. It had been salvaged from a defunct local dance pavilion whose oddly shaped lumber had proven inadequate for the construction of a traditional dwelling.

Added to this, Miles was a talented inventor. Over the years he had earned a reputation for remarkable ingenuity as he fascinated friends and neighbors with a wide variety of unique contraptions—everything from bamboo croquet sets to children's amusement rides. This pair of boats was the latest novelty in his repertoire.

Predictably, the people of Encinitas had looked on curiously as Miles had begun laying out the boat ribs, and they had speculated about what new surprise was in store for them with the apparently ordinary-looking crafts. They were not disappointed. Curiosity gave way to astonishment as, with each new stage of their construction, it became increasingly clear that these were no ordinary boats. In fact, they were the most unusual boats that anyone had ever seen. They were not seaworthy at all, nor, for that matter— and this was the greatest shock of all—had Miles ever intended them to sail. Rather, they were houses built in the shape of boats, perfect residences for nautically minded landlubbers.

The Boathouses were the fulfillment of a long-cherished dream. Ever since his days growing up along the shores of Lake Michigan, Miles had longed to build a large boat of his own, and he had nearly achieved this goal as a young man when he had received an invitation to join a band of missionaries sailing to Central America. Family obligations had stood in the way, however, and he had been forced to turn down the opportunity.

But Miles had never forgotten the lost trip to Central America—or his dream of building a boat. For the next thirty years, he had continued to dream without any apparent hope of this dream becoming a reality.

Until now.

FAST-FORWARD NINETY YEARS, AND it is October 12, 2019. I have joined several other descendants of Miles Minor Kellogg to celebrate the listing of the Encinitas Boathouses on the United States National Register of Historic Places. It is a momentous occasion, not only for us but also for San Diego County.

Ever since the Boathouses' construction nearly a century ago, they have numbered among the county's most iconic landmarks. Each year countless tourists drive out of their way from historic Coast Highway 101 to marvel at the SS *Encinitas* and SS *Moonlight*, to photograph them and to quiz local residents about the origin of the boat-shaped cottages. So highly valued are the Boathouses that in 2008 the Encinitas Preservation Association (EPA) organized their purchase for over $1.5 million[*] to ensure that they would never meet a fate similar to that of many other beloved historic buildings[†]— being razed to the ground by real estate developers and replaced by modern Southern California mansions. The EPA's achievement in securing the Boathouses' place on the prestigious National Register is a further potential safeguard because they are now eligible for tax incentives and grants or loans to fund maintenance and some much-needed restoration work.

Halcyon weather casts a benediction on the event. It is a cheerful, sunshiny autumn morning, the sky blue and clear, and a faint scent of brine wafts up and over the nearby cliffs from the Pacific Ocean, freshening the air. As my relatives and I cluster on the outskirts of the small crowd gathered in front of the Boathouses, I imagine how, on a similar day almost exactly ninety years ago, my great-great-grandfather must have laid out the Boathouses' ribs right where we are now standing.

As this image floats through my mind, I turn to a cousin, Miles James "Jim" Kellogg.

"Jim, what do you think your grandfather would have thought about all this?" I ask, gesturing toward the few hundred local residents who have willingly given up a Saturday morning to pay homage to their town's most notable attractions.

Jim, Miles Minor Kellogg's namesake, never knew his grandfather. But he did grow up hearing his own father talk about helping in the Boathouses' construction, and he himself has followed in the footsteps of generations of Kellogg woodworkers. Whether or not he is aware of it, he likely has an instinctive understanding of the workings of his grandfather's mind.

There follows the briefest of pauses as Jim glances about him, taking in the cameramen, politicians and other dignitaries. "He probably wouldn't 've come," is his terse assessment. "I think he was like my dad—humble."

I have to swallow a chuckle. Knowing what I do about the Boathouses' history, I am certain that at least one other factor might have influenced Miles to stay away from this commemoration of his handiwork. The Boathouses had still been taking shape in late 1929 when a local news editor had poked

---

[*] Included in this purchase was an apartment complex that Miles built directly behind the Boathouses.

[†] Among these was Miles's almost equally remarkable chalet-style log cabin, made from telephone poles.

fun at them. Capitalizing on Miles's well-known Christian faith, the editor had seized the chance to sell a few extra papers by likening the Boathouses to Noah's ark. Miles, to say the least, had not been amused. But the fabricated story was too good for other periodicals to pass up. Soon it had ballooned into one about an eccentric "second Noah" who had built the Boathouses in anticipation of an imminent second worldwide flood. The story spread throughout the country, and Miles was still battling his reputation as a builder of arks at the time of his death a few years later. Even today, after the passage of nearly a century, the "ark" nickname sticks to the Boathouses like glue.

Nevertheless, Jim has undeniably captured the essence of his grandfather. In terms of both his background and his life philosophy, humility was Miles's defining characteristic. And it was humility, in both senses of the word, that, accompanying every milestone of his life, had led to his decision to build his famous Boathouses. Humble circumstances—that is, poverty—had dogged his footsteps from early childhood. It was poverty that had taught him to make do with whatever materials came to hand and that had fostered his natural penchant for creativity.

Frugal (and modest) as he was, Miles, I am convinced, would have been astonished—if not scandalized—by the outlay of money that the affluent, modern city of Encinitas has raised to preserve the two cottages that he fashioned inexpensively from recycled lumber. Such an exorbitant amount of money, he might very well have insisted, would have been put to far worthier use in feeding the hungry or sheltering the homeless—acts of charity that he consistently engaged in throughout his life.

As I researched for this book, I could not help but recognize a connection between Miles's practice of recycling—that is, finding a use for materials that others might have discarded as worthless—and the love that he demonstrated to his fellowmen. Just as he found a purpose for the tired, old wood from the Moonlight Beach Dance Pavilion, so too did he recognize a value in every person he met. No one was beneath his notice. No one too old, too poor or too unattractive to be deemed without value or usefulness. In essence, throughout his life, Miles Minor Kellogg strove faithfully to "act justly and to love mercy and to walk humbly with [his] God" (Micah 6:8, NIV). And it is this legacy that I cherish more than any other.

Rachel Brupbacher

2021

1
LAYING THE FOUNDATION

Necessity, it has often been said, is the mother of invention. And necessity was a commodity that the backwoods of nineteenth-century Michigan offered in abundance, providing its native sons with ample opportunity to hone diverse skill sets. Miles Minor Kellogg was one of the most remarkable innovators it ever produced. Throughout his life, Miles would distinguish himself as an architect, builder, businessman, carpenter, homesteader, inventor, musician and homespun poet. He was, consequently, always far too busy to pass on many family stories, and it fell to his relatives to leave behind precious scraps of information for posterity to piece together again into the crazy quilt that is his life story.

Miles came from pioneering stock on his father's side. In the early 1800s, his grandparents Minor and Mariah Kellogg had joined other adventurous men and women in abandoning the overpopulated American Northeast to settle what would ultimately become the State of Michigan. Minor and Mariah had raised their family in the eastern part of Michigan's Lower Peninsula* before relocating permanently to its northwestern region. There, in Leelanau County, they had claimed a homestead near the shores of Lake Michigan—the vast expanse of water that would define their grandson's first quarter century.

---

* According to the 1850 Census, Minor and Mariah were living in Washtenaw County, which adjoined Livingston County, where a distant cousin, John Preston Kellogg (the father of Dr. John Harvey Kellogg and "Cornflakes King" William Keith Kellogg) had settled.

Joining Minor and Mariah in Leelanau was their son Justus, Miles's father. Justus had recently returned home from the Civil War[*] and was soon to be divorced from his first wife. In 1862, Justus took advantage of the Homestead Act passed that year and filed on a 160-acre homestead that adjoined his father's.

In contrast to the Kelloggs, Miles's maternal forbears boasted a seafaring heritage. Following his move to Leelanau, Justus married a beautiful, young French-Canadian woman by the name of Christiana Thebo.[†] The Thebos had allegedly been well-to-do in their native France, where Christiana's grandfather (so it was said) had been a prosperous shipbuilder.[‡] The Thebos, however, had evidently failed to bring their prosperity with them to the New World. Christiana's father, Emmanuel, worked as a carpenter and shipbuilder, but his career commanded a far more modest living than his father's had. Perhaps to augment his income, Emmanuel also served at one point as first mate aboard a commercial trading ship that sailed the Great Lakes.

Christiana's aristocratic appearance and bearing fostered her son's faith in stories of family grandeur. Dark-haired, blue-eyed and extremely petite—she never weighed more than eighty pounds or stood more than four feet six inches tall—Christiana was an elegant and attractive "woman of domestic talent and social refinement."[1] She was also a natural caregiver. Despite a crippling childhood injury, which left her lame in one leg, she consistently epitomized Christian charity by being "neat and industrious, and a great help to her neighbors. She would help them with their sewing, and [was] always on hand to help in case of sickness in the neighborhood."[2]

Christiana's natural talent for nurturing lent itself well to motherhood. She became a warm and loving mother to the two sons she raised with Justus: Emanuel Porter (known simply as "Porter"), born in 1867, and Miles Minor, born on June 8, 1870.[§]

Outwardly, the brothers could not have been more different. While Porter resembled the stocky Justus, Miles took after the French side of the family, inheriting his mother's dark hair and striking blue eyes, along

---

[*] Various reasons, including so-called seasonal disorder, were recorded for Justus's discharge from the Fourth Michigan Infantry after only a few months in the service.

[†] Some sources give her name as Anna Augusta Thebo.

[‡] Miles would always cling to stories of ancestral wealth. Over the years, he would frequently voice his expectations of an inheritance one day coming from relatives in the old country—expectations that would, regrettably, remain unrealized.

[§] Through their father's dissolved first marriage, Miles and Porter had three older half-siblings: Frank, Amelia and Herbert.

Justus and Christiana Kellogg. *Author's collection.*

with his seafaring grandfather's passion for the water. Nevertheless, both boys would be equally shaped by their early experiences on the family homestead. Their childhood, as Porter revealed in a letter years later, was rustic and colorfully primitive:

Father built a one-story house 24 x 24 feet. It was divided into two rooms: a living room and a kitchen. And he cut 16-inch stove wood and filled the front room full of wood. He had about ten acres cleared, so he planted some Hubbard squashes, potatoes, and other vegetables and raised some food for the winter months and then started for the lumber camp a hundred miles or more from home to work for wages of $1.50 per day of eleven hours of hard work and board, also bunk filled with straw and two blankets.

So Mother was left alone with her two boys. I was about six years old and my brother Miles Minor three years and ten months old. I remember somewhat of that winter. Our spring, which furnished us water in summertime, was froze over so we couldn't get water from it. So Mother opened the windows and broke icicles and melted them in the wash boiler for domestic use. The snow was so deep one could not see an eight-rail fence, which is about four feet six inches high.

A man by the [name of] Burdick…owned a general store located three miles from our home. His stock of goods consisted of groceries, dry goods, hardware, tinware, graniteware, paint, patent medicine, farming equipment, and the post office and was called Burdicksville. One morning Mother said, "I have filled the stove with wood and closed it up tight so it will keep a fire until I get back home so don't touch the stove while I am gone. I am going to Burdicksville. I hope to get a letter from Father." So Mother, a little woman, a cripple, started out for Burdicksville, plodding through the deep snow, and received her letter from Father. Those were days of toil and hardship.

Grandfather owned a good farm. All the stumps and roots were removed, and the farm was in good condition. He had a large log house with a large fireplace in the center of the rear end of the large living room. The opening of the fireplace was four feet high and six feet wide, with a crane on each side for the brass kettles. The one on the left side was for the hot-water kettle, and the one on the right had two kettles. She did all her cooking and baking in those two brass kettles. The last time that I was in Grandmother's home, she had bought one of the first cook stoves made in those days. It was called the elevated oven cook stove. It was placed at the side of the fireplace, and the stovepipe connected to the fireplace chimney.…

There was a large hay and granary barn and outbuildings (log-constructed buildings)—poultry house, corn crib, smokehouse where they smoked ham and bacon. The poultry consisted of chickens, geese, ducks, turkeys, guinea fowl, also a pair of peacocks.

There was an abundance of wild fruit (blackberries, raspberries, grapes, strawberries, currants, and plums), nut-bearing trees (walnuts, beechnuts, hickory nuts, also hazelnuts), and wild game (deer, elk, black bears, and gray wolves), also fur animals.

When they cleared the land in those days, they left standing all the best sugar-maple trees, which furnished shade for stock, also around the house. When they made maple sugar, they chose a shady place for the boiling pan, and that was a woman's job to make the maple sugar.

When they cleared the land, they left standing a few trees such as the hickory tree. It is a strong-grain timber used for making wagons, also tool handles, such as axe handles. Also, white ash—it is a straight-grain timber—from which they cut three-foot logs, which they split into ¼-inch thick shakes for covering the roofs of their buildings. That was before shingle-making machines were invented.

My grandfather had a few sheep, and Grandmother would card and spin the wool yarn and bought the warp. Her oldest daughter lived six miles from Grandmother's home. She had a loom, and Grandmother would walk that six miles to weave the wool yarn into cloth to make blankets and clothing. And [in] all the making of garments the sewing was done by hand. There were [no] sewing machines in those days. And [she] made her own candles, which furnished the light by which she knitted stockings and gloves.[3]

It was likely the poverty of the hardscrabble homesteading life that prompted Justus to give up his acreage when Miles was still a toddler. Around 1873, he moved his small family down the coast to a town called Ludington. Located on the edge of vast pine forests, Ludington was a hub of logging activity and was fast becoming a major shipping port on Lake Michigan. Justus, who occasionally worked as a carpenter and house painter, was able to secure employment as a shipbuilder in Ludington and, for a time, at a sawmill in the nearby village of Buttersville.

Miles would always cherish pleasant memories of the next thirteen years. In a nostalgic poem that he wrote in middle age,* he described gentle pastimes typical of a rural upbringing—skating in the winter, swimming

---

* See page 114 in chapter 11.

Christiana Kellogg (née Thebo). *Author's collection.*

and sailing in the summer, playing in the sawmill where his father worked and learning the three Rs at the little local schoolhouse.

Music, too, enriched Miles's early years. On his father's side, he was descended from generations of musicians. Back in Leelanau, the extensive Kellogg clan had been so well known for its singing talent that, even decades later, neighbors would still rapturously reminisce about the beautiful "angel voices" that they had once heard coming from the various Kellogg homesteads. Justus, a fine singer in his own right, passed on this gift to Miles, who not only sang beautifully but also learned to play the organ, piano and violin.[*]

Yet Miles was destined to associate Ludington and Buttersville with painful memories as well. It was there that the most tragic event of his life took place—the death of his adored little mother. Christiana had been suffering from tuberculosis when, around 1885, she died after accidently swallowing a dose of worm medicine. Miles, then about fifteen years old, was left unspeakably distraught. Before his mother's body was laid into the ground, he salvaged a few last keepsakes—a bunch of flowers and bits of cloth and braid from her burial gown—which he clustered together and carefully preserved. Consistent with the sentiments expressed in what became one of his favorite songs—Harry Kennedy's "A Flower from My Angel Mother's Grave"—Miles treasured these mementoes to the end of his days.

A Flower from My Angel Mother's Grave

> *I've a casket at home that is filled with precious gems,*
> *I have pictures of friends dear to me.*
> *I have trinkets so rare that came many years ago*
> *From my far-distant home across the sea.*
> *But I've one little treasure that I'll ever dearly prize,*
> *Better far than all wealth beneath the wave.*
> *Tho' a small, faded flower that I plucked in childhood days,*
> *'Tis a flower from my angel mother's grave.*

---

[*] As an adult, Miles would also play the clarinet in a Modern Woodmen of America band in Boulder, Colorado.

Treasured in my memory, like a happy dream,
Are the loving words she gave.
Still my heart fondly cleaves to the dry and withered leaves,
'Tis a flower from my angel mother's grave.

By the sweet ties of love forever blest
In the still and silent night, I often dream of home,
And the vision ever tells me to be brave,
For the last link that binds me to that home I love so well
Is this flower from my angel mother's grave. [*]

A bleak year followed Christiana's death. By its close, her husband and sons, seeking consolation for their loss, had decided to join her family, the Thebos, in their adopted hometown of Benton Harbor, about 150 miles south of Ludington.

It was there in Benton Harbor—bolstered by a supportive and secure community of many aunts, uncles and cousins—that Miles, now about sixteen, gradually came into his own and began to seek ways of bettering himself.[†] Due to both financial necessity and a lack of opportunity, his education had been stunted—limited to the level of the third grade—but he was ambitious. Refusing to let circumstances dictate his fate, he tried to make up for the deficiencies in his formal schooling by becoming a voracious reader. Typical of the times, his self-directed course of study included the Bible, of which he became a "deeper than average student."[4]

But Miles's interest in the Bible was not strictly academic. As a young boy, he had always willingly and happily attended church services. Now, soon after his arrival in Benton Harbor, he became a lay minister in a local Church of God.

Miles's decision to align himself with the Church of God was a remarkably independent one, especially for a teenager. Any religious instruction that he had received at home from his French-Canadian mother had presumably been fundamentally Roman Catholic. Similarly, few of the Thebos would have encouraged his involvement with a Protestant denomination. Nor were his father's religious preferences apparently responsible for inspiring

---

[*] A very old and incomplete family transcription of the verses.

[†] Miles's grandfather Emanuel Thebo lived with a daughter and son-in-law. Miles's grandmother Rosalie Thebo had been committed to the Michigan Asylum for the Insane in Kalamazoo for an unknown psychiatric malady.

The earliest known likeness of Miles Minor Kellogg. Standing at right, he is pictured with an unidentified relative. *Author's collection.*

Miles to join the Church of God. When Justus died a couple of years later, his funeral would be conducted at a Baptist church.[5]

The decision would also have a tremendous impact on Miles's future. Although initially catalyzed by a thirst for education and a need for solace following his mother's death, Miles's participation in church affairs was not a shallow, short-lived means of self-pampering. He took his faith extremely seriously and would remain ardently devout for the rest of his life. Moreover, within just a few short years, his passion for his faith would lead him to make two further decisions that would alter the course of his life forever—his marriage to Ruth Jane Wood and his conversion to Seventh-day Adventism.

2

LOVE IN THE FARAWAY

Water—more specifically, the Great Lakes—unquestionably played a defining role in Miles's ancestry and his upbringing, just as it would in his future decision to build boathouses. But the Great Lakes played yet another crucial role by connecting him to his future wife long before they ever met. While he spent his boyhood summers sailing on Lake Michigan, a little girl was reveling in the flowery fields and woodland of the Canadian countryside not far from Lake Ontario.

Ruth Jane Wood, the daughter of a New York farmer, grew up in a household not unlike her future husband's—one that was well acquainted with poverty but that nevertheless brimmed over with contentment. In her memoirs, Ruth would express gratitude for the happy childhood and strong moral and practical upbringing that her parents, Lewis and Malinda, had given her. She observed, "They were always so good to us and tried their best to please us in every way that was right. I am glad that they taught us how to work and to be neat homemakers, and to be clean in mind and body."[6]

Lewis and Malinda taught by example, daily instilling in their many children a value for cheerfulness, industry, integrity and modesty. Above all, they demonstrated an unflagging spirit of generosity. They freely shared whatever they had with anyone in need, regardless of how much or how little they could afford to spare.* Ruth fondly described her father

---

* Such generosity was inspired by personal experience with privation. Lewis had grown up in poverty in Schoharie County, New York, the son of a farmer-cum-woodcutter and his wife, an "herbal doctor" and midwife.

Malinda Wood. *Author's collection.*

as "always an industrious and hard-working man, meeting misfortunes cheerfully, and was a man well liked by all who knew him. He was always jovial and made friends easily."[7] Moreover, he was "unselfish" and "would give his last cent to help someone in need, and many have been grateful to him for this." Ruth admired this same spirit of generosity in her mother, remarking that she had "never known [her] to turn anyone from her door who would come for food."[8]

In light of his general spirit of goodwill, it would be tempting to conclude that it was Lewis's inborn love for his fellowmen that prompted him to turn draft dodger during the Civil War, prior to Ruth's birth. The truth, however, is less inspiring. Malinda had been a young widow with two small children when she married Lewis in 1858, and when Fort Sumter was fired on a few years later, she immediately made up her mind that she was not going to lose a second husband to war. It was at her urging that Lewis fled north to Canada with her and their family of boys.[*] They settled in Sunbury, Ontario, just across the St. Lawrence River from New York.

---

[*] These were Ruth's older brothers—Frank, Foster and Mel—and her older half brother, Will Ball. From her mother's first marriage, Ruth also had an older half sister, Emma, who remained behind in New York.

Life in the quiet, quaint village of Sunbury was idyllic—so much so that the Woods chose to remain in Canada long after it was safe for Lewis to return to the United States. While Lewis worked as a tenant farmer, Malinda tended the house and raised their sons. She also gave birth to three more children, all daughters: Mary Esther (known as "Ett"), Ruth Jane and Margaret Ann (known as "Annie").

Ruth, named after a godmother, was born on March 7, 1871, and was christened in a local Methodist church. Her recollections of life in Sunbury would always remain startlingly clear, and in later years, she would paint a delightful picture of her early childhood:

> *My memory still goes back to that little home village with its green meadows and clear running brooks which I had to cross on my way to the little red schoolhouse. I can remember the road into Kingston as the schoolhouse was near this road. There was also a large cheese factory not far away. People would leave the milk in large cans on stands along the road and men from the factory would come to get them....*
>
> *I enjoyed going to school. We had good teachers and many nice schoolmates. One of my chums was a Quaker girl. She had good Christian parents, and many times my parents and I went to Quaker meetings in the little schoolhouse....My sister and her sister were also close friends. I believe that the sweet Christian influence of these Quaker associates had quite an influence in my life....*
>
> *I surely did enjoy reading from the large charts they had for children in the first grade then. I can also remember the cards the teachers gave us on the last day of school. I memorized some of the poems on mine. One was such a pretty card with a picture of the Shepherd carrying his staff and leading his sheep. I think that we had wonderful school books in those days. As I grew older I read and reread my sister's third reader, and can still remember many stories and poems in it....*
>
> *In my memory I can see the rail fences and the pretty woods not far from our house, and the beautiful wild flowers. Many times I went with Mother to gather wild blackberries and huckleberries in these woods. Even if we did have to climb rail fences to get there, we were well rewarded by pails of berries. Mother would gather peppermint, catnip, pennyroyal, and many other kinds of herbs. She would dry them and put them away in paper sacks for future use as medicines. The doctor lived twelve miles away and we didn't have any automobiles then. She also gathered juniper berries which are very good for neuralgia. Mother was a good, industrious woman, and*

Father was always busy. Men didn't get good wages in those days, but with planning and looking ahead, and with patient toil, they made a good home for us and we were all happy together.

In the evening when all was quiet we could hear the whippoorwill singing his evening song in the woods. All kinds of birds and harmless animals made their homes in the pines. Sunbury was a quiet home-like village. It seems as if it must have been something like those villages where Jesus used to visit. I was just as happy and interested then with the pretty wild flowers and old-fashioned gardens as I am today. My father enjoyed gardening and always had a good garden of vegetables as well as flowers.

In Canada the 12th of July was a holiday, and we children would always go out to the main road to see the parades. Mother trimmed our sunshades with different colored crepe, twisted together and put around the crown, and one time we had our hats trimmed in the Canadian colors, and when the men in the parade came by they saluted us.[9]

As pleased as the Woods were with life in Sunbury, though, they were not destined to remain in Canada forever. Around 1878, Lewis took a trip out west to visit his mother and siblings, who had settled in Minnesota, near a little town called Plainview. Impressed by the region's prosperity and encouraged by the vast network of relatives who could lend a helping hand, Lewis made up his mind to stay and promptly sent for his wife and children to join him there.

Malinda and the children, attached as they were to Sunbury, at first greeted his decision less than enthusiastically. However, they changed their minds upon seeing Plainview for themselves. Ruth, then about seven years old, adapted easily and instantly fell in love with her new home:

We children enjoyed our journey from Canada to Minnesota, both by boat and by rail. We were very tired and lonely when we arrived at our destination. Father had a house and everything ready for us, and all our cousins and other relatives were glad to meet us.

Minnesota was a great farming country. It was a beautiful sight to see the large fields of waving grain, corn, and the lovely gardens. My father was truly a great farmer and he enjoyed his work. He and my brothers worked hundreds of acres of land. We had nice horses, cows, calves, chickens and turkeys roaming the green pastures. All our animals, even the cats and dogs, were well cared for. My parents were lovers of animals, and so were we children.

Ruth with her father, Lewis Wood, around the time of the family's move to Minnesota.
Author's collection.

I often long to hear again the mowing machine cutting down the sweet-smelling hay. Then would come a harvester, cutting down the golden grain, and then the threshing machine. We would have a crew of about twenty-five men. Father and my brothers would exchange work with the neighbors. It took lots of men and work to thresh all kinds of grain and to get it ready for the market and the mill. Annie and I often went with Father to the mill to see the wheat ground into flour, the corn into meal, buckwheat into pancake flour, and we would bring the bran home for feed for the cows. Father always enjoyed taking us along with him on these trips.

I enjoyed my school days in Minnesota too. We had to walk about two miles to school, but we enjoyed walking along the green fields and stopping now and then to pick wild roses and other flowers for our teacher. In the winter when the snow was too deep for the horses and sleigh to get through we would walk right over the snow banks which sometimes covered the fences. We enjoyed skating on the large pond next to the schoolhouse. We young people of the community had many happy times together sleigh-riding on moonlight nights, over the snow behind a chain of frisky horses, with the sleigh bells ringing out through the crisp, cold air. We lived five miles out of the town of Plainview, and we didn't have any automobiles in those days, so we had Sunday school and all our entertainments in the schoolhouse. All my cousins were musical, and some were music teachers and schoolteachers. Many of our evenings were spent in singing and in playing the organ....

My grandmother was a great comfort and pleasure to us. She made her home with her youngest daughter. They didn't have any children so it was quiet there. Once in a while she would go to visit each one of her sons and daughters. We were always glad when she came to stay with us for a couple weeks....She would tell many wonderful stories of different cities in the state of New York.[10]

After ten happy years in Plainview, Ruth naturally expected to spend the rest of her life there. Her father, however, had other ideas. Once all of his sons were married and established with homes of their own, he discovered that he could no longer farm on the same large scale that he had been accustomed to doing. As a result, he became an easy target for real estate agents from Benton Harbor, Michigan, who convinced him to purchase a fruit farm there. Around 1888, to the great dismay of his family, Lewis left for Benton Harbor and then sent for Malinda, along with Ruth and Annie, to join him.[*]

Ruth, now seventeen, did not adjust as easily to a move as she had done before. A long time elapsed before she could yield to Michigan's natural splendors and wholeheartedly embrace her new home:

I was very lonesome, and also sick on account of the change of climate. I believe I had a touch of malaria. The neighbors were all good to us and tried to keep me from getting too homesick....[One good neighbor] used to take me for rides and try every way to cheer me up....

After I got over my sickness I really enjoyed it there....It rained during the summer, and the trees were beautiful. When we first went there we lived

---

* Ruth's brother Mel and his wife accompanied them.

in a new house belonging to the man who ran the boarding house where my father had stayed until we came, but after a while we moved over to another place just a short way from town. This was a large three-story house with a large veranda all around the front. There were all kinds of fruit trees there—pear, peach, apple, cherry, and all were in bloom at various times and it certainly was a beautiful sight. Not far away was a grape vineyard, and below the hill was a little lake. Then there were acres and acres of strawberries, black and red raspberries, blackberries, etc. This indeed was a beautiful and prosperous fruit country.

Sister Annie and I with our friends used to love to wander through the beautiful lanes shadowed with flowering trees. We young people used to get on the large boat and go over to St. Joe and come back on the streetcar or ferry boat. We didn't have to pay to ride that far on the large boat, and only five cents on the ferry or streetcar. Benton Harbor and St. Joe were called the twin cities. I used to like to stand on the bluff at St. Joe and watch the large boats coming into the harbor. I could tell by the sound of the whistle just which boat was coming into Benton Harbor.[11]

Although not mentioned in her memoirs, a reason besides homesickness and physical illness exacerbated Ruth's initial despondency. She was mourning a lost romance, which she immortalized in a poem, "I Met Him in the Faraway"*:

I met him in the Far-away
Yet lovely northern land.
He crossed my life in youth's young way
And won my heart and hand.

The hour he sought me for his bride
My heart can ne'er forget.
But, ah, full soon he left my side
To be a young cadet.

He said his faith would long outlast
The glittering stars above,
And while the hours went speeding past
He sang me songs of love.

---

* Written on Sunday, July 27, 1890, in Benton Harbor, Berrien County, Michigan.

Though thought may fill the eyes with tears,
Love rules my being yet,
And o'er my heart while flit the years
Still reigns the young cadet.

But Ruth's heart was soon to be mended. As it happened, her pleasure in watching for the steamboats was prophetic. Unbeknownst to her, as she stood on the bluffs, listening to the boat whistles, her life was to shortly become entwined with that of a young wheelsman aboard one of the large vessels. Two years after her arrival in Michigan, a new romance was waiting just around the corner, and her life would never again be the same.

3
A MARRIAGE OF TRUE MINDS

Choosing a life companion was not a matter that Miles took lightly. He was scandalized by the knowledge that his father's first marriage had ended in divorce, and he had every intention of avoiding the mistakes of the previous generation. Complicating the situation was the fact that Benton Harbor did not offer limitless opportunities for courting. Despite a population of several thousand, the town was largely rural, and respectable social gatherings where unmarried young people could meet and mingle were few and far between, typically confined to church services and church-sponsored outings. It was at one such event that Miles first laid eyes on his future wife in late 1890.

At the age of twenty, Miles had already established himself in two separate careers—one on land and one on water. With a background poor in funds but rich in woodworking traditions, he initially had had little choice but to follow in his father's footsteps and become a carpenter. As luck would have it, he was uniquely suited to the career. He possessed not only an aptitude for working with wood but also an immense drive that would characterize his entire professional life. Miles was just seventeen when he built his first house, a bachelor residence for himself, his father and his brother.[*] Within two years, he was advertising his services as a carpenter and builder in Benton Harbor's *Weekly Palladium* and helping erect an enormous pontoon bridge, one that he—the only man in the district to volunteer for the job—would subsequently paint singlehandedly.

---

[*] Soon afterward, he built a second house, a cottage, where he would begin his married life.

Nevertheless, Miles's first and greatest love was the water. From the moment of his birth, he had seldom been separated from Lake Michigan by more than a few miles. Consequently, before settling down to carpentry for good, he decided to try his grandfather Thebo's way of life. His first job was as a ship's carpenter, but by 1890, he was working as a wheelsman aboard a large steamboat called the *Mabel Bradshaw*.

It was while he was away on the *Mabel Bradshaw* that year that his father died. Porter had married a couple of years earlier, but Justus, allegedly disparaging his young daughter-in-law's housekeeping abilities, had chosen to live with Miles instead.* One early summer's day, Justus heard three calls of a whippoorwill, then regarded to be an omen of death. Justus, revealing a sensitivity for premonitions that his descendants would inherit, prophesied his own death in three days' time. The prophecy, tragically, held true. When Miles returned home, he found his father dead from a stroke and buried.[12]

It was around this difficult time that Miles's path crossed Ruth's. With grief and loneliness acting as bonding agents—Ruth was still nursing a broken heart from her lost romance—the two young people gradually struck up a warm friendship. Years later, Ruth would reminisce about their meeting and courtship:

> *One evening my sister and her gentleman friend and I went to a large hall to attend a revival meeting. We enjoyed the meeting, and later attended when they moved over to the Church of God. There was a young man there leading out in the singing, and the minister in charge asked him to lead in prayer. He seemed to be an earnest Christian young man, and I admired him from the first, although I did not know who he was. Annie and I went to church there quite often after that.*
>
> *One Sunday I happened to be at a friend's home and was surprised to see this young man come there. We were introduced, of course. We played the organ and sang, and our friend asked the young man to sing "The Flower From My Angel Mother's Grave." When I mentioned that I had to be going home, he said he had to go that way, and asked if I had any objection to his walking that far with me. Of course I had no objections as my friend had told me what a fine young man he was.*
>
> *Well, he seemed to like me from the first. I don't think he had noticed my sister and me at church. We were good friends for some time, going to church and prayer meeting together, but never to dances or shows or other*

---

* Porter was also apparently living in Grand Rapids by this time.

places of worldly amusement.... We were very happy together, wandering through those beautiful lanes.

Friendship ripened into love, and on the evening of his 21st birthday, June 8, 1891, I, Ruth Jane Wood, was married to Miles Minor Kellogg... We were married in the house he had built.[13]*

On the day of the wedding, Ruth found the cottage thoughtfully prepared for her arrival. It was filled with furniture that Miles had personally handcrafted for their new life together. Miles, inspired by the happy hours that they had spent singing together and by memories of the music that had filled his boyhood home, also presented his bride with a brand-new pump organ.

Marriage inevitably brought changes for both of the newlyweds but especially for Miles. Not only did he have the responsibility of providing for a wife, but also his days on the Great Lakes came to an end. Ruth, fearing for her husband's safety, was less fond of the water than he was. Bowing to her wishes, Miles returned to dry land and found employment in a local carpentry shop.

But 1891 held even more in store for Miles. That year was to completely transform his religious life by bringing about his personal introduction to Seventh-day Adventism.

First established thirty years earlier in Battle Creek, Michigan, the Seventh-day Adventist Church was an outgrowth of the Millerite movement, whose adherents had believed that Jesus would return in 1844. The Adventist Church, already unique among Protestant denominations for its observance of Saturday as the Christian Sabbath and the emphasis it placed on the Second Coming of Christ, was further distinguished by a health message that advocated vegetarianism and adherence to Old Testament dietary laws.

It is possible that Miles had already been familiar with Adventism for some time through his extended family. By the 1890s, the Adventist Church had acquired a significant following in Michigan, especially in Battle Creek, where John Preston Kellogg, a distant relative and devout Adventist, had settled and where two of John Preston's sons, Dr. John Harvey Kellogg and William Keith Kellogg (the "Cornflakes King"), ran the Battle Creek Sanitarium.[†]

---

* According to the wedding announcement published in Benton Harbor's *Weekly Palladium* on June 12, 1891, a certain Reverend Wm. H. Prescott officiated at the ceremony. Family notes indicate that he was affiliated with the local Church of God or Church of Christ.

† Miles and Dr. Kellogg considered each other relatives. During a conversation about their respective family trees, they concluded that their fathers had been second or third cousins. Current research, however, points to a more distant connection.

It was the magnetic effect of the Adventists' music, though, that actually drew both Miles and Ruth to the denomination. Seventh-day Adventist evangelists had been holding meetings in Benton Harbor on and off for several years when, in the summer of 1891, Miles and Ruth began attending a series of lectures with Ruth's parents and Miles's sister-in-law. Ruth later wrote:

> *Two Adventist evangelists, Elder Frank* [Hutchins] *and Elder Richardson, together with their singing evangelist, Charles P. Whitford, came to Benton Harbor, put up a large tent, and started a series of lectures. We would go down on Sunday nights, and we began to really enjoy the preaching and the singing. Brother Whitford had a beautiful voice. My father said he could stay there and listen all night to his gospel songs. Finally* [Miles] *became so interested that he went every night....I, like many people, could not see that Saturday was the right day to keep. Elder* [Hutchins] *and his wife came to call on us often, trying to get me more interested.* [Miles] *was studying his Bible every Sunday and evenings after work. He used to go over to the minister's home and they would give him Bible studies, and they also gave studies in our home.*[14]

Miles's interest in Adventism grew swiftly. That fall, just months into their marriage, he and Ruth attended an Adventist camp meeting in Lansing, Michigan, where they heard sermons from the Adventist prophetess, Ellen Gould White, and Adventist minister John Norton Loughborough. Miles even lent out their new organ to provide music for the meeting. Ruth, however, took longer to unreservedly accept the Adventists' message. She would recall, "[Miles] was quick to learn and understand. I was proud of him....Well, at last he decided to keep the Sabbath, and of course wanted me to also, but I couldn't see it that way then."[15] Miles was baptized around 1893 in an inlet or outlet of Lake Michigan called the LL Gap or Double L Gap. Another year passed before Ruth also came to "accept the truth" and made the decision to be baptized, along with Porter's wife, Emily, in the St. Joseph River.

From this point forward, the Seventh-day Adventist Church became the focal point of Miles and Ruth's lives. Miles, far from a passive believer, threw himself into personally serving his denomination with his professional talents. With the assistance of other local church members, he erected the first Seventh-day Adventist church building in Benton Harbor around 1894.[16] He also worked on Dr. Kellogg's world-famous Battle Creek Sanitarium.

Benton Harbor's first Seventh-day Adventist church, built by Miles Minor Kellogg, circa 1894. *Author's collection.*

In exchange, the Seventh-day Adventist Church offered the young couple previously undreamed-of opportunities. Miles made such a favorable impression on the Benton Harbor evangelists that before the tent meetings closed Frank Hutchins urged Miles to consider a career in the ministry. Hutchins, who had recently accepted a mission assignment in Central America and was undoubtedly anticipating the usefulness of a ship's carpenter on his Caribbean travels, also asked Miles to accompany him abroad as tent master.

Miles found the invitation extremely tempting. If he accepted, he could not only be of active service to his church, but he would also have an excellent excuse for fulfilling one of his personal ambitions—building a boat of his own, one that, in this case, would ferry his family and the

Right: The first family portrait: Miles and Ruth with Chester and baby Irma. *Author's collection.*

Below: The train depot at Sodus. *Author's collection.*

40

missionary group throughout the Caribbean. But Miles was forced to decline Hutchins's request. Ruth had no desire to move so far away from her parents, and Lewis and Malinda had no intention of parting with their daughter.

As his family responsibilities began to mount, Miles realized that he had made the right decision. His and Ruth's first child, a son they named Chester, was born on June 27, 1892, just a year after their marriage. Four months later, they left Benton Harbor for the neighboring township of Sodus,[17] where Miles built a new house for his little family on a ten-acre farm that adjoined that of his parents-in-law. There they welcomed their second child, a daughter they named Irma, three years later on July 3, 1895.

Ruth was enchanted by the pastoral life on the farm, which reminded her of her happy childhood years: "It had a nice apple orchard.... [Miles] set out some small fruit trees, strawberries, etc....It was such a pretty place....This home was surrounded by beautiful fruit trees, and we enjoyed walking through the orchards when they were in bloom. We were near the banks of the St. Joe River, and by just crossing the road and standing on the bank we could see the large ferry boat passing by on its way to Berrien Springs."[18]

Miles and Ruth continued to be active in church affairs. Among other things, they lent out their little organ to evangelists who held meetings along the St. Joseph River. Ruth later expressed her fervent hope that the organ "was the means of helping to bring someone nearer to the Master" at these meetings.[19] It was also in Sodus that they made the acquaintance of another young Adventist couple, Charles and Edith Shell, with whom they forged an enduring friendship. The Shells had married the same summer as Miles and Ruth, and Charles, a clerk in his father's store in Sodus, was the same age as Miles. Together, the two young men engaged in active church work, both in Sodus and Benton Harbor.

So pleasantly situated, Miles and Ruth could not have asked for a more promising start to their married life. Nor could they have ever imagined leaving the snug little community of Sodus. Nevertheless, unforeseeable circumstances would soon compel them to abandon their lovely farm and embark on an odyssey that would take them ever farther westward.

Miles would not see his native state again for thirty years.

4

BUILDING, BIRTHING AND BURYING

ll too soon, tragedy shattered the tranquility of life in Sodus. In the summer of 1895, just days after Irma's birth, Ruth's beloved sister Annie died suddenly of diphtheria in Chicago. It was a blow from which Ruth would not quickly recover.

Annie's death had other far-reaching consequences as well. Lewis and Malinda, prompted by their loss, decided to move back to Minnesota to be near their other surviving children. Reluctant to leave their daughter and grandchildren behind, they urged Miles and Ruth to go with them.

Miles's initial reaction to the request was ambivalent, at best. He was contented in Sodus and relishing his church work. There was little incentive, as far as he could see, for exchanging Michigan for parts unknown to him. However, his love for Ruth, coupled with her glowing accounts of her Minnesota childhood, eventually tipped the balance in favor of them packing up and departing with her parents.

To Miles's relief, life in Minnesota turned out to be quite similar to the one he had always known. Before long, he was busily engaged in construction work and had built two houses for his growing family, one in Plainview and one three miles from town. It was in one of these houses that Ruth gave birth to their third child on November 22, 1896. Baby Edith, named after Edith Shell, was a "very good natured" and "cute, fat baby girl" who had "big, blue eyes and dark hair" like Miles.[20]

But life in Plainview did present some drawbacks. Most significant was the absence of a flourishing Seventh-day Adventist community. Miles,

Left: Annie Wood. *Author's collection.*

Right: Three little Kelloggs. Clockwise from top: Chester, Irma and Edith. *Author's collection.*

having grown accustomed to living among like-minded believers, found this change disconcerting at first. Nevertheless, he quickly recognized in this apparent disadvantage a prime opportunity to engage in self-directed lay evangelism. He had just turned twenty-six when, in August 1896, he began holding a series of local lectures about Sabbath keeping and advertising them in the local paper.

Other troubles were not so easily remedied, however. Not only did Miles and Ruth both dislike Minnesota's cold, harsh winters, but also Ruth was deeply unwell. Two years earlier, when they had still been living in Michigan, she had been a patient at the Battle Creek Sanitarium.[21] Now she was suffering from similar complaints but without access to comparable care. Miles began to look for an alternative place to settle.

He did not have to look long. Porter had moved to Boulder, Colorado, and was now tempting his brother and sister-in-law to join him and his family by raving about Boulder's great natural beauty, its warm climate, its fresh mountain air and its excellent work prospects. Seconding Porter's enthusiasm were the Shells and Ruth's sister Ett Pogson, who were all planning to relocate to Boulder with their own families as well. Yet a further incentive was Boulder's thriving Adventist community. Since the arrival of

Porter Kellogg with Mary, his second wife. *Author's collection.*

the first Adventists at the foot of the Rockies a quarter century earlier, the Adventist Church had become well established in Boulder. Moreover, it was Boulder that Dr. John Harvey Kellogg had selected as the site for a new branch of the Battle Creek Sanitarium. The doors of the Boulder-Colorado Sanitarium had opened just that year, 1896.

Miles and Ruth ultimately found such inducements impossible to resist. In March 1897, they packed up their small family and headed west for Colorado with Ett and her children.

In financial terms, they could not have made a wiser decision. Much of modern-day Boulder was as yet undeveloped, and the construction company that Miles and Porter established was an almost overnight success. The brothers were soon building one house after another.[*]

Further securing Miles's financial footing was an ever-widening array of side ventures. Whenever he was not building with Porter, he undertook carpentry jobs at the many mines at Louisville, southeast of Boulder. He installed the supports in what was known as the "old Sunnyside mine" and built its tipple and tower. Miles also became a partner in a grocery business, and he owned a used furniture store and a "health place" (a gym with a pool). Another enterprise was a concession of boats—likely built by Miles himself—which he rented out at "Valmont Lake," a reservoir northeast of Boulder.

Not all of Miles's ventures turned out well, however. A business partnership that he entered into with Ruth's brother-in-law Will Pogson ended acrimoniously. He and Will had jointly purchased a mill in the mountains with the intention of eventually relocating it closer to town. When the time came to move it, Miles, who felt that he had a prior obligation to complete a carpentry job, hired another man to help Will in his stead. The hired man proved incompetent, and the mill overturned, bringing about a long-standing rift between the brothers-in-law.

Nor was everything well at home. Colorado's more hospitable climate did nothing to improve Ruth's health. To the contrary, she became chronically ill almost from the moment of her arrival in Boulder. At one point, her condition was so critical that she had to be hospitalized at the "San."[†] Miles, possibly as partial payment for his wife's medical bills, did maintenance work on the Boulder Sanitarium's elegant multistory main brick building[22] and erected some of the smaller cottages on the Sanitarium grounds.[23]

---

* Miles, either by himself or in collaboration with his brother, also built houses in Denver.

† The precise nature of Ruth's ailments is unknown. However, her daughter Dorothy indicated that Dr. Kellogg operated on her mother's "ligaments." This would have been at either the Battle Creek Sanitarium or the Boulder Sanitarium.

This page and opposite: Two of Miles's Boulder houses. *Author's collection.*

Exacerbating Ruth's health problems were the family's frequent moves throughout town and her recurrent pregnancies. Miles, ever thrifty, would install his wife and children in one of his newly finished houses, only to move them out—and usually into a far less sophisticated dwelling—as soon as it sold. In the midst of these many moves, Ruth delivered five children within just eight years: Walter, a "dear, good-natured little baby"[24] boy, on January 11, 1899; Vera, a "sweet baby girl" who was "born with two little white front teeth"[25] on July 15, 1900; Francis Murl (known simply as "Murl"), a "cute, fat little boy"[26] on February 1, 1902; Helen, a "rosy-cheeked, chubby little girl,"[27] on March 9, 1903; and Lloyd, another "cute little boy,"[28] on June 24, 1905.

Chester, who was not quite five years old at the time of the move to Boulder, later described the incessant hustle and bustle that characterized the family's eleven years there:

> *Our first stop, a temporary one, was at the home of a Pease family on East Pearl Street, diagonally west across the corner from Beasley Ditch, an irrigation canal....*
>
> *From the Pease place, we moved up to what is now about Third Street, on West Arapahoe. It was a rough, undeveloped area of cactus, sagebrush, and boulders. The Farmer's Irrigation Ditch flowed below the house site; and Boulder Creek was below the ditch. Our domestic water was carried from it.* *Our Aunt Ett Pogson lived with us there. Velva, older than I, and*

---

* A small waterfall formed to the left of the house in the wintertime. Silica in the water made the family ill.

The Sanitary Hotel. Miles and Ruth are seated on the porch, holding Irma and Edith, respectively. Chester is seated at the top of the steps. *Author's collection.*

Walter were her children. We did not live there many months. A "twister" came out of Boulder Canyon and wrecked the house. Fearing that this might recur, the families had moved [into] the home of one Charlie Shell, several blocks to the east of our home. The house was never rebuilt.

About this time Papa and a Mr. Jensen* purchased an abandoned ore-sampling building, on West Pearl, north side, near 9th Street. This they remodeled into a rooming house, and called it Sanitary Hotel. We had an apartment on the east side, first floor. There was a bakery in the basement, underneath it….

While we were resident in the Sanitary Hotel, Papa had purchased lots on Grove Street, between 17th and 18th on the south side of the street. On the back of the 18th and Grove corner, he built a shop and a barn. They extended full-width of the area. The barn, with a hay loft, accommodated the bay and gray team, and the family cow.…

Down east on Goss Street, in the 2200 block, were several nice lots, providing a small orchard, rich garden soil, and spare building space. Here, the head of the family built a frame, gambreled roof home. There were four rooms on the first floor and two on the second. In addition to the house, there were a shop, barn, and later west towards 17th Street, a grocery store

---

* George Jensen, also a Seventh-day Adventist.

building. Papa was a partner in the business for a time. The other partner,
a Mr. Clark, took over later....

From the near-ideal home on Goss Street, we moved to a new home near
Fourth Street, two or three blocks north of the Boulder Sanitarium. It was
another gambrel-roofed structure. It was one of others which Papa built in
that area. One of these was for Uncle Will Pogson and Aunt Ett....

Papa continued in his construction, in various areas of the city. I cannot
recall his being among the unemployed....When we moved from North
Boulder to a small, slab-built temporary home near Fourth and Arapahoe
Streets, [Mama] *had a long spell of illness. While living in that little shack,*
Father was busy down on 15th Street—at the end of Grove Street. Here he
built a row of three commercial units, with the first and second floor residential
apartments in one. For a time we lived in the first-floor apartment....

From there we moved directly west a city block, to Fourteenth Street,
between West Arapahoe and Beasley Irrigation Ditch. On the west side
of the street, Papa built a shop-barn, into which we moved and remained
while our new home on the front of the lot was in construction. This was
a two- or three-bedroom house, with kitchen, bathroom, dining room, living
room areas. It was heated by a coal-burning hot-air system.[29]

Besides the precarious state of Ruth's health, a series of personal tragedies, commencing with the death of one of the children, deeply shook the entire family. The summer after his birth, Walter contracted whooping cough and died, aged just seven months, in the early hours of August 3, 1899. Edith, then not quite three years old, was so sensitive to her parents' heartbreak that she never forgot her baby brother or the family's somber buggy drive to the burial: "He had blue eyes and a real light complexion....he was so sick and my aunt stayed there....all night with my mother, and [he] died....I went with them to the cemetery....I was the next youngest, so I sat between my mother and father on the front seat."[30]

Walter was laid to rest near a stream in Boulder's Columbia Cemetery. The Sanitarium chaplain, Elder Francis Wilcox,* conducted the funeral service. Wilcox touched Ruth by describing Walter as "the sweetest little flower that he had seen for many a day," and she would speak gratefully of Wilcox ever afterward as having been "a great comfort to us in our sorrow."[31] Ruth never ceased to grieve the loss of her baby, but she showed a brave front to her other children, telling them with confidence, "Some day the little boy will be back in my arms."[32]

---

* Wilcox subsequently became editor of the Adventist periodical *Review & Herald*.

But Walter's death was not the only cross that Miles and Ruth had to bear. Two years later, they mourned the passing of their good friend Charles Shell. The Shells had come west to Boulder specifically in the hopes of restoring Charles's failing health. These hopes were sadly disappointed, and the Shells returned to Michigan, where Charles died soon afterward at the age of only thirty-one.

Further grief followed a few years later with Miles's bitter split from the Seventh-day Adventist Church.[33] When he and Ruth had first arrived in town, they had eagerly embraced the opportunity to join Boulder's vibrant Adventist community. By 1903 or 1904, however, Miles's participation in church affairs had dwindled significantly.

This apparent change of heart could be explained several ways, foremost of which was a storm that was then raging in the Adventist Church. The 1890s and early 1900s were marked by great controversy and conflict for the church, especially where Dr. John Harvey Kellogg was concerned. The doctor's alleged pantheism (or belief in the presence of God in nature), his continued criticism of Adventist leadership, his prolonged disagreement with the church over its control of his Battle Creek Sanitarium and his deteriorating relationship with Adventist prophetess Ellen White would culminate in his expulsion from the church in 1907.

The Boulder Sanitarium. Miles did maintenance work on the beautiful edifice. *Author's collection.*

According to Chester, Miles was essentially an "idealist" and a "Kelloggite," and such discord within the church undoubtedly had a demoralizing effect on him. Confiding in his minister son years later, he would voice support for Dr. Kellogg's controversial views. He would also express a dissenting opinion concerning the authenticity of the Spirit of Prophecy, or the belief in Ellen White's divine inspiration. Although Miles agreed with Chester that White was a "good writer," he believed her to be "no more inspired than the best writers of today."[34]

It was at this delicate stage in Adventism's history that some gossip questioning Miles's own altruism in church work caused him to permanently sever his ties with the denomination. Chester, who was then enrolled in the local church school, later wrote, "He owned property in Niwot, a few miles northeast of Boulder. Several lots, a small house, a feed mill, and a blacksmith shop constituted the town property. This, to assist in the construction finance of the new church, Papa contributed to the project. As the story goes, in my memory, it was whispered among the gossipers, [that the property] 'would not have been so freely given, if Brother Kellogg did not expect to get the construction contract.'"[35]

This was not the first time that Miles's church community had disillusioned him. Earlier, he had dammed up a swamp and converted it into a pond for the local church. Although other congregation members had pledged to help finance the project, none of them had ever reimbursed him for his labor or for his outlay of money. As far as Miles was concerned, the elders' gossip was the ultimate insult.

His reaction was all too predictable to those who knew him well. As an idealist and incurable perfectionist, Miles held himself—and others—to extremely high standards. This ordinarily admirable trait, however, tended to give rise to a hypercritical outlook; the intense frustration that Miles felt whenever any of his ideals were disappointed often caused him to be childishly petulant and impulsive in expressing his disapproval.* When the church elders approached him with plans for the new church building, expecting him to do the work for them, he refused to even look at the blueprints. He betrayed his wounded feelings by angrily informing the elders

---

* Miles's reactive behavior could alienate him from some of the people he loved best. During the early years of his marriage, he had torn up his mother-in-law's chicken pen after he had failed to mend it to his satisfaction. On another occasion, when he had returned home a day ahead of schedule and found Vera in the bed that he shared with Ruth, he had yanked his daughter out of the bed, bellowing, "No one sleeps where I sleep!" Not surprisingly, the children tended to shy away from him for fear of incurring his wrath, and Ruth's warning that she would "tell Papa" if they misbehaved was usually enough of a threat to keep them in line.

that they could "go to h—l."[36] He then perversely added that if they were true representatives of Christianity, he would rather "take his chances going to the 'other place.'"[37] With that, he gave up his membership in the Seventh-day Adventist Church forever.

Miles's decision instantly upended his family's way of life. Pulling Chester out of the church school, Miles enrolled all of the children exclusively in public schools from this point forward. Church attendance ceased, and religious talk at home likewise ebbed away. Chester would later recall, "After Papa left the church, there came a gradual change. As the family increased, Mama's family burdens, as with Papa's financial ones, became heavier. All spiritual life faded out. The Sabbath was never mentioned."[38]

Yet try as Miles might to eradicate his association with Adventism from his memory, it had left an indelible impression on his psyche. To the end of his days, he would continue to proselytize to friends and neighbors about Adventist interpretations of biblical prophecies. In time he would also renew the practice of Sabbath keeping. Most significantly of all, Adventism had sown the seeds of inspiration for what would become known as the crowning achievement of his building career.

HOMESPUN HAPPINESS

Family feuds, health crises, betrayals, deaths—it sometimes seemed to Miles as if he ran a gauntlet of heartbreaks and setbacks in Boulder. But ironically enough, it was also in Boulder that he enjoyed some of the happiest and most prosperous years of his life. His successful building career, besides guaranteeing financial security, allowed everyone in the family—from the ever-busy head of the house down to the newest baby—to delight in countless everyday pleasures and, on occasion, to experience the thrill of a heart-stopping escapade.

Even Ruth would one day look back on the Boulder years with comparative pleasure. This was due largely to the support and comfort that her older sister, Ett, provided. Practical and feisty, Ett had only two children of her own to look after and was able to help the long-suffering Ruth with her household chores. Ett also served as a second mother to her large brood of nieces and nephews; she never hesitated to speak her mind where their welfare was concerned, especially since Ruth was too soft-hearted and too physically weak to mete out corporal punishment as needed. Both Ruth and Miles, who clearly approved of his sister-in-law, were too grateful for Ett's help to object to what others might have considered "meddling."

But the disciplining was not left to Ett alone. Although work frequently called him away from home, Miles took his family responsibilities seriously, and he would punish his children if they disobeyed. Chester remembered a whipping he received as a five-year-old: "One of the impressions made in my early life…was a sound thrashing administered by my father.

A family portrait, circa 1905. Standing at back: Edith, Irma and Chester. Front row: Murl, Ruth (holding Lloyd), Vera and Miles (holding Helen). *Author's collection.*

He had built a beautiful skiff (small boat of about 12 ft. in length) and anchored it temporarily in the canal. I had violated strict orders to 'stay out of the boat.'"[39]

On the whole, however, instances of corporal punishment tended to be few and far between. Miles was fearful of turning into an excessively strict disciplinarian like his brother. Porter dispensed corporal punishment liberally and was all too ready to believe the worst of his children, especially his daughters, worrying about their behavior to the point of paranoia. Miles, who deeply disapproved of Porter's methods, was determined not to copy his brother's mistakes. He never raised a hand to his own daughters, and it was not until Chester was fifteen that he again whipped his oldest son. Chester recalled:

Four miles east of the city, Boulder, the "Gem of the Rockies," boasting 365 days of sunshine in the year, was Valmont. This was a beautiful rocky eminence rising out of the plain. Nearby was a popular ball field. On a particular day an important game was to be played. I planned to be there with a friend or two. Now, Irma and Edith planned to go somewhere and asked for Tom* and the buggy. To both of us Papa replied, "I'll see." Fearing that he would not favor me with his "I'll see," I took off, and had a good time. In the evening of that day, the parental eye looking into mine was accompanied with a stern, "I'll take care of you, young man." You know, I thought it was coming then, but Papa took off on business for the evening. How I suffered mental torture for the next three or four hours! I knew that "I'll tan your hide" was sure in coming. I preferred it while in my trousers, rather than in my nightgown. Sleep got the best of me. I had to go to bed, and did. Almost at the same minute Papa appeared.

"All right, come with me," and to the backyard I followed. Leaning against the wall was the same buggy whip that we carried, needlessly, for old Tom. Standing at the effective end of that whip was an impressive experience. After all these years I seem to hear the windy "zing" and feel the stinging coil of that instrument of education. There was never again a boyhood open disobedience—that Papa was aware of, or that I can remember.[40]

Any discipline that Miles administered was also balanced by the affection that he showed his loved ones through his thoughtful gifts and actions. In fact, perhaps his greatest accomplishment during his years in Boulder were not the many houses he built but the numerous gadgets and tools that he

---

* The family horse.

developed, most of them specifically intended to bring joy to his children or to ease his wife's burden. Among the most noteworthy contraptions were a washing machine for Ruth, clothespins that gripped in proportion to the wind's strength, a sugar bowl with a spoon through the lid and a hatchet fitted with a clamp so that it cut shingles efficiently.*

Through his handiwork Miles became a hero in his children's eyes. They adored playing guinea pig for his inventions and loyally insisted that he could "do anything he set his mind to."[41] In the wintertime, they would skate on the pond that he had dammed up for the church and use his handmade sleds to slide down Boulder's University Hill, a district that was becoming increasingly built up with his houses. At a time when automobiles were a new and exciting sight, the braver children would ask passing motorists for permission to hitch rides behind their vehicles. After one car pulled them on their sleds for a couple of miles, the children would hitch rides back with another driver.

Miles's creative flair also guaranteed that Christmas, a holiday near and dear to his heart, was always a special occasion. Each year he faithfully handcrafted a personalized toy for each of his many sons and daughters. This tradition made one Christmas all the more memorable. At school that winter, Irma had contracted diphtheria—the same disease that had carried off Ruth's sister Annie so quickly—and, according to Edith, all was chaos at home:

> There was no chance Santa would want to come to [our] home that year. There was a great big quarantine sign on the front of the house. Why, the neighbor had even tied her little boy to a tree to keep him from coming to this "pest house"!....No, Santa would not want to come this year. And Papa…was away from home. Mama had her hands full trying to care for sick children. She had to watch the ones who might be getting sick, too, and keep them from exposing the neighborhood children. Little Murl had already slipped out of the house and gone running down the street.
>
> Usually there was a Christmas tree, one [we] would get [ourselves] in the mountains behind Boulder…but Papa was gone and everyone sick or quarantined. [We] had not even hung up the traditional sox which each year before had held a large orange in the toe.
>
> But when Christmas morning dawned, and [we] children came down the stairs, certain the plate of goodies [we] had put out for Santa "just in

---

* The design for this hatchet was subsequently stolen. When Miles invented it, he did not have the necessary funds to take out a patent. A so-called friend did and took out a patent for it in his own name.

case," would not have been touched, what a lovely sight met [our] eyes! The big family table was set with fruit at every plate, and by each plate a gift for each child! It turned out to be one of the nicest Christmases ever! Caring neighbors had brought over a food basket for the invalids, appreciated by all but the proud eldest son! And Papa had come home. Christmas was very important to him. It was he who had made the lovely gifts for his children. There was a toy cupboard for one of the girls, a doll couch for another, and for Vera a doll dresser.[42]

Miles's generosity extended to those outside the family as well. He and Ruth were both kind-hearted, and they would never turn away anyone in need. Ruth became so well known for her philanthropy that vagrants were said to "mark" her house as a way to signal to other men who were down on their luck that they could find a hospitable refuge there. Edith recalled, "Each tramp who came to town knew he could get a warm meal at her house."[43] Miles and Ruth were equally hospitable to needy local children and, from time to time, would take in an extremely poor little girl named Hermine Dahler.

But while the Kellogg home might have seemed like a safe haven to passing drifters and starving children, it was not free of danger. The Kellogg children, especially the younger ones, often produced fireworks inside the house—sometimes literally. Several times Miles returned home in the evening to find scorch marks throughout the house. Although his culpability could not always be proven, Murl, the family's resident firebug, would inevitably fall under suspicion. One night, a lamp caught fire; the house would have burned down if Irma had not had the presence of mind to fling it out the window. Another time, it was the kitchen curtains, and Edith saved the day by throwing a large container of water onto the fire, dousing it before the fire wagon arrived.

Usually, though, there was no doubt whatsoever about Murl's guilt. The Kelloggs had recently moved into an unfinished house when the little boy discovered some shingles in an upstairs room and set them alight. Another day, he ignited the base of some wallpaper downstairs; before the fire engines could arrive, the fire had run straight up the paper, all the way to the second floor, where Irma lay ill with diphtheria. He began yet another fire when he discovered a pile of shavings that his father had carelessly left lying on the floor, half-hidden from view behind the family piano.

Nor was it exclusively through his pyromania that Murl kept the family on its toes. He was only a toddler when he met with a nearly fatal accident.

The house (*at right*) where the lamp caught fire. *Author's collection.*

Chester recounted, "Returning from shopping one day, Mama and one of the girls stopped by the sidewalk in front of the apartment. They had driven to town in the top buggy. Baby Murl, seeing Mama, ran to meet her and got in between the front and back wheels. Tom, anxious to go to the stable, started to move. Down went Murl, and the rear wheel rolled over his fat little belly. We thought that he was seriously injured. However, he was immediately scrambling to his shaky little feet, uninjured."[44]

The older children, meanwhile, experienced narrow escapes of their own. One day, the two oldest girls were walking along a creek when Irma fell in. Edith was unable to pull her sister out of the water, and a stranger, who had seen Irma fall from a distance, had to come to the rescue. A similar accident occurred when Vera stumbled into the creek. Murl, for a change, played the hero by fishing his sister out by the skirts. Through yet a further watery adventure, Chester taught Edith a rough lesson in survival. Brother and sister were out in one of their father's rental boats in the middle of Valmont Lake when Chester decided that the time had come for his little sister to learn how to swim. He picked up Edith without warning and dumped her overboard, giving her only the simplest of instructions: "Stay in there and swim!"[45]

Apart from such dramatic episodes, however—or perhaps because of them—the Kelloggs generally enjoyed a happy and contented life in Boulder, and since Miles and Porter were succeeding in business, they might have remained there indefinitely if two catastrophic events had not conspired to

The Kellogg children on their beloved Old Tom. *Author's collection.*

force them from Colorado. The first blow fell with an economic recession, which was exacerbated by a nationwide economic downturn.* Carpentry work in Boulder became scarce. The second and more devastating blow fell around the same time, when Miles lost almost all of his valuable property, including a recently acquired ranch, through fraud. Chester explained:

> *Papa exchanged the 15th Street property for 320 acres of land on a branch of the Platte River, near Fort Morgan, Colorado. There was a misunderstanding over the real estate dealer's fees. Papa's regular attorneys were not free to take the case and recommended another firm. Not having financial resources, he temporarily turned over the property deed for security. Papa was ready to reimburse the firm for their legal services; and seemingly*

---

* The Panic of 1907, also known as the Knickerbocker Crisis.

over a lengthy period failed in an endeavor to obtain the return of his deed to the Fort Morgan property. Briefly, the lawyers had forged Mama's name to legal papers and recorded the transaction in approved legal procedure. Papa was advised by his regular attorneys that the only way out was a shotgun, which they did not recommend.[46]

For Miles, an honest man who expected honesty from others and who had been beside himself a few years earlier at his fellow church members' unjust accusations, it was perhaps the shaking of his trust in his fellowmen, rather than the actual loss itself, that was the more distressing.* As for his children, although they never grasped the finer details of the fraudulent transaction, they felt its effects keenly. Fifteen-year-old Chester, in particular, was all too conscious of how the swindle affected his family's future, and he never recovered from the loss of what would have been a beautiful—and perhaps permanent—country home. In old age he wrote, "Having taken the long trip down to the ranch with Papa, how I had longed, in my boyish mind, to live on that ranch on the Platte. The disappointment won't go away, to this day."[47]

---

* Miles and Ruth both made a point of impressing the importance of honesty on their children.

6
THE WILDERNESS YEARS

T he attorneys' fraud spelled unequivocal financial disaster. Miles
had lost more than the lovely ranch. He had lost, in the bargain,
practically all of his other assets—real estate that he had acquired
over a decade, literally by the sweat of his brow. For the moment, he still
had employment doing mine and residential construction work in nearby
Lafayette and Louisville, but due to the economic recession, Boulder and
most of its neighboring communities had ceased to be lucrative places in
which to ply his trade.

When a fresh start beckoned in the north, he was quick to respond. In
fact, desperation made him inadvisably hasty. According to Chester, "About
this time the U.S. Government opened S.E. Wyoming for homestead entry.
Papa took a few days off, went to the Land Office in Cheyenne, and filed on
a quarter section, half-way between the towns of Burns and Egbert, on the
Union Pacific Railroad, and about one and a half miles north of that line.
Lodgepole Creek ran past the S.W. corner of the property. The land was
rolling, and cultivatable only in small areas. Much better land was available;
but Papa had left a crew on the Louisville works and had to get back."[48]

When Miles made his entry for the land in Laramie County on August
8, 1907, he was making a commitment to cultivate it for the next five years.
He was also following in the footsteps of his father and his grandparents,
who had filed on their own homesteads in Michigan nearly half a century
earlier. Yet there was an outstanding difference: With Lodgepole Creek as
the only nearby natural water source, he would be attempting a particularly

challenging method of land cultivation—dry farming, or agriculture without irrigation—on his 160 acres.[*]

Ruth, meanwhile, was expecting their ninth child. Miles, upon selling their latest Boulder residence, a comfortable little cottage, had moved his large family into a five-room house next door—one without any form of insulation. Even with the warmth given off by the kitchen stove and heater, the house was often bitterly cold. It was here that Ruth delivered her baby, a daughter they named Dorothy, on January 25, 1908.

Miles had been waiting just long enough for the new child to arrive. Two days after Dorothy's birth, he set off for the homestead, with Chester in tow, to start work on a dugout. It was an experience that his teenaged son would never forget:

> *Papa and I hitched up Tom to the single-horse farm wagon, and started on our trip to the homestead, less than 100 miles north. It was quite a trip. On the way we slept out on the ground and/or in the wagon box. It was a three-day journey; and to me it was adventure.*
>
> *Having arrived, we set up housekeeping in the open, tentless, and went to work. For the first two rooms, about 16 feet apart and parallel, we excavated back into the hillside. These we walled up from stone from the farm; and we shed (flat) roofed them. The lower side came down to near grade level. The front was of frame construction. The two rooms were connected by an eight-foot wide section—stone back and frame front.[49]*

The rest of the family followed five months later in the spring. While Miles and Chester transported the household goods from Boulder by horse and wagon, Ruth and the younger children traveled north by train. Located in Wyoming's southeastern-most county, the town of Burns (then known as Luther) was little more than a whistle-stop. The large family's arrival in the tiny community made an impression, especially on one local man.

After watching one child after another descend from the train, the man finally asked, "Is that all?"

"Yes," Ruth responded sweetly. "Don't you wish you were one of them?"[50]

Miles would eventually build a frame house onto the dugout. Chester wrote, "By a year or two, a living room and large kitchen were built onto the front of this first structure. They were plastered—ceilings and sidewalls; and openings were trimmed."[51] Edith described it as "a nice house, connected

---

[*] According to Miles's testimony and that of his neighbors, only 120 to 140 acres were cultivable.

Wyoming neighbors. *Author's collection.*

to the rooms of the dugout that had been finished off into two bedrooms, warm because they were partly underground—one for the girls and one for the boys."[52] The family had no indoor bathroom facilities and had to use an outhouse, with pages from old Sears & Roebuck catalogues serving as toilet paper. Miles, who usually slept at his carpenter's shop in Burns, ultimately improved the property by building a windmill to pump water up from a well and installing plumbing to the house.[53]

In later years, Chester would voice support for his father's decision to turn homesteader, remarking, "Economically, it was a sound move—the best way out of near to nothing."[54] But Wyoming was far from a land flowing with milk and honey. Although Miles labored diligently on the homestead, planting potatoes, corn, wheat, oats and millet as feed for the animals, the harvests that he reaped from the twelve to fifteen acres that he cultivated could not have been termed outstanding successes. Moreover, these harvests, partly as a result of drought, became poorer by the year.

Not even Miles's professional skills could offset the homestead's meager profits. Initially, he received a small burst of commissions for various building projects in and around Burns, including the construction of the town's water tower, but Laramie County's sparse population could not supply him with the steady number of contracts that he needed to support his family. Faced with few other choices, Miles resorted to a controversial form of employment—strikebreaking.

Strikebreaking was an unpleasant—and frequently dangerous—yet viable way of earning a living for dry farmers during the harsh winter months when funds at home sank low and their labor was not absolutely required on their homesteads. It was during one such stretch of "scabbing" that Miles was inspired to write a couple of long odes to his philosophical ideals. A rugged individualist to the core, he eschewed aligning himself with any organization other than the Modern Woodmen of America and clung defensively to his right as a "free citizen of the good Old USA" to seek employment where he could without accounting to anyone. He saw himself as the quintessential "common man":

I am working in the car shops of the Great M.P.,*
Handling bolts and washers and putting in new keys,
A-laying on my back with my shoulders in the snow,
Handling bars and wrenches until I nearly froze.
Every morning with the bunch I go and check in my time
And then go walking up the track until it's dinnertime.
From seven in the morning until 5 o'clock at night,
With my eyes chuck full of embers and my clothes with grist alight.
Although we are but souls earning our bread and butter,
A-working at jobs that once was another's,
We are all free citizens of the good Old USA.
We will work for whom we please if suited with the pay.
We are a jolly crowd. The bosses all are good.
They would pay us better wages, we are certain, if they could.
We care not to run the church or dictate to capital's power.
The poor receive the kingdom. The sick will have their hour.
Be patient, then, my brother, and strive to do your best,
And, when the airship is perfected, we will all go home to rest.
We will need no more the coaches, engines or boxcars.
We'll get aboard the airship and sail right up to Mars.
And, if the pilot should lose his compass or something else go wrong,
We would come to Earth a-whooping. We would sing another song.

I am stopping at the Dry Farmers Hotel
On East 11 St., the place by the strikers is known very well.
It's here you can meet many distinguished guests:
Mr. Corn Flakes† and Molasses and Paky Swift‡

---

* The Missouri-Pacific Railroad.

† Presumably William Keith Kellogg.

‡ Meatpacking baron Louis F. Swift.

And Mr. S.J. Wilson, who for short we call Sam.
He makes a noise in his sleep like a young German Band.
Also Mr. J. Erickson who handles the hammer—
He will go back to the ranch when it gets warmer.
Mr. Phoenie Arizona has gone from our midst.
With sorrow we remember the things that he did.
He has gone back to the Ranch because it got warmer.
There's Mr. Molasses.
We know he's not sick by the food that he musses.
He has surely not lost his good appetite
For the amount he consumes each morning and night.
There our Paky Swift with whom the strikers would like to shake hands,
But for their company he don't care a d—n.
A-coming home at noon not many days since—
Instead of going round the corner he jumped over the fence.
Mr. Mooney, for him we feel sad.
The strikers call him names, and then he gets mad.
Oh, dear Mr. Mooney, hold on to your mouth.
Whatever they say, just let it pass.
And Mr. Fred Hill who comes home and says he is sick
But he is courting the cook. Now ain't that a great trick?
We surely do know what's all of his trouble.
He'll be all right when he gets doubled.
And last, but not least, is the cook with a pair of brown eyes.
*We are surely delighted with her fine bread and pies.**

Despite Miles's best efforts, the family was soon leading an increasingly hand-to-mouth existence. Thus began what the Kelloggs, in sympathy with the Israelites who left Egypt, came to dub their "forty years in the wilderness."[55] Chester outlined the first two difficult years:

> *In March I commenced plowing on a ten-acre area along our south line. In May we had a very heavy snowstorm. For protection I brought Tom into the shack with me. That first year we had 12 acres in garden varieties, and corn and millet for stock feed.*

---

* On another page, Miles compiled a list of people who then figured prominently (and often negatively) in the news—some of the same people to whom he referred in the poem. Misspelling several of the names, he wrote "S.J. Willson," "William Talge," "John S. Sanders, Jr.," "E.E. Mooney," "James Christinsun," "Fred Hill" and "Miss B.M. Willson" (Bird May Wilson, female lawyer and suffrage worker).

Fuel was at the high price of $7.50 to $8.00 per ton. We could afford little, for money was on the short end. We drove over the prairie picking up cow chips, and I drove for miles along the railroad line picking up coal that had rolled off the cars. To adapt ourselves to the necessity of the situation, Papa built a sheet iron stove with a deep fire box to accommodate the cow chips....Mama considered it very [impractical], and had me replace it with her cast iron range. We managed to use coal thereafter.

My personal recollection is that we had come to experience the lowest level of financial resources for providing the necessities of living. We had a good roof over our heads, but little for the stomach, and a shortage of proper clothing. Well, we came through.

Father found work among the homesteaders. He, also, superintended the construction of a very large barn for an old-time rancher. A Mr. Wisroth. And then directed the moving of this man's ranch house, several miles over the prairie to a location near Pine Bluff. Papa's age reached 40 years while we worked on that project. Forty years! An old man, I thought. Also, he built the residence of Mr. Sibley, the banker in Burns.

After a time carpenter work became scarce. We built a shop on the west side of the street running north, down the hill from the railroad station. Here we made concrete chimney block and brick, did small carpenter jobs, filed saws, etc. I worked occasionally for Victor Smith, foreman of the Carper Ranch, adjoining us on the west. For a few months I was employed with the Union Pacific Railroad as section hand. We removed decayed ties from under the rails, and replaced them. We worked in pairs, twenty ties made a day's work of 9 hours. But the pay was good—$1.15 for the 9 hours. Carpenter's wages, at the time stood at $4.00 for eight hours.

The banker decided to build a telephone line running from Burns to Carpenter on the Colorado border. It was a one-wire grounded system. For poles to support the line, eight-foot 2" x 4" were spiked to the farmers' fences along the road. From Burns to the Kellogg Homestead and on to Egbert, we used the upper wire of the wire fences. I built the line for Mr. Sibley....

There were rattlesnakes everywhere—along the trail to school, in the house yard, the barnyard, and pastures. It seems that we met most of them in the first two years.[56]

Life on the prairies inevitably entailed recurrent battles with the natural elements, especially in the wintertime. Every year, the Kelloggs found themselves at the mercy of life-threatening blizzards. According to Chester, "It was not the three or four inches of snow that were the matter

Two of the Kellogg girls by the flooded Lodgepole Creek. *Author's collection.*

of danger; but the ferocity of the wind driving that snow to near suffocation and invisibility. I was once lost, carrying two pails of water from the well, within a few feet of the house door. And these storms came up suddenly, catching sheepherders on the open range, and horse-drawn vehicles on the roads, often within short distances from shelter."[57] Making matters worse was the monotony of the Wyoming landscape. In fair weather or foul, the absence of trees and mountains to serve as landmarks could make the prairies disorienting.

Such hazardous weather conditions posed a particular threat to the school-aged children, who had to trudge a round trip of several miles to attend the school in Egbert. The children—usually poorly clad, with only pieces of cardboard to cover the holes in their shoes—frequently fell prey to the mercurial whims of Mother Nature. Sometimes the only way they could find the route home was by feeling their way along the barbed wire fences. A fear of these blizzards was never far from Miles and Ruth's minds. Both of them were old enough to remember the horrifying reports of the Schoolhouse Blizzard that had struck the plains states years earlier, in 1888, and claimed hundreds of lives. Many of the victims had been children struggling to make their way home from school.

It was only a matter of time before Miles took matters into his own hands and found a way to shorten his children's walk to school. Around 1910, he and Chester erected what became known as "the little Kellogg schoolhouse." Chester explained, "Of course education was not only a privilege, but a necessity. Papa made a deal with the State Department of Education. We deeded one acre of the northwest corner of our ranch. State provided material costs and the teacher. Papa and I did the construction."[58] Miles designed the "Kellogg schoolhouse" on skids so that it could be moved whenever necessary, and it was initially positioned at a location central to all of the neighboring families. A local girl named Vida Hall became the children's beloved teacher.

A concern just as grave as the children's safety, however, was the quagmire of depression into which Ruth was rapidly sinking. She had felt the downturn of the family's fortunes more keenly than anyone and had not been prepared for what a homesteading life involved. Back in Boulder she had puzzled over the "buffalo chips" that Miles mentioned in his letters home. She had not been in Wyoming long before she discovered that they were the recycled waste products of buffalos or cows and that they would serve as the family's main source of fuel on the treeless prairies. Her recollections of life in Wyoming would not be pleasant:

> *I didn't like it in Luther. We could look for miles and miles and see nothing but prairie. There were two farmhouses not far from where we lived that had some trees around them. They had been built for several years. We lived*

Outside the Kellogg schoolhouse: Helen (*second from left*), Vera (*fourth girl from left*), Murl (*seated forward on pony*) and Lloyd (*far right*). *Author's collection.*

The schoolhouse entrance. In doorway: Edith and Irma. Middle row: Murl (*second from left*), Helen (*second from right*), Vera (*far right*). Front row: Lloyd (*center*). *Author's collection.*

four and a half miles from Luther, and I believe two or more from Egbert, another small town….

There was a church and a high school at Luther, and a post office and a few stores. There was also a post office and a few stores in Egbert….

We had good neighbors, some very nice refined people who had left their good homes and come there. Some were lawyers, ministers, and businessmen….Many have nice homes now with little groves of trees around their places. They need the trees, for the wind certainly did blow when we lived there.[59]

Ruth's poor eyesight intensified her depression. When she had contracted the measles as a small child, she had not been kept away from the light, and she had been left partially blind as a result. This handicap had subsequently become a source of relentless frustration for her. Much to her mortification, whenever Miles would call in to her to ask for the time, she had to climb onto a chair and put her face directly in front of the clock to read it. Miles, whose own vision was unimpaired, was not always sympathetic. At times he became irritated if Ruth, who was otherwise an immaculate housekeeper, failed to notice little things like buttons that had fallen onto the floor or if she missed sweeping a small patch of dirt. In Wyoming, what little eyesight Ruth was left with had scant beauty to feast on. The desolate landscape, with its unvarying topography and sparse vegetation, was a far cry from the glorious gardens and orchards that she had reveled in as a girl.

Further fueling Ruth's sense of hopelessness was the lack of good fellowship. Her social circle had been considerably wider in Boulder. There she had enjoyed the company of her sister Ett and, before Miles's split from the Adventist Church, the support of a church community. In Wyoming, by contrast, neighbors were few and far between, and the homestead's distance from town made regular church attendance prohibitive.* Miles and Chester benefited from the distractions of work and social interaction, but Ruth was condemned to spending most of her days on the lonely homestead with only the children and her increasingly morbid thoughts to keep her company.

Bereft of beauty, close friendship and spiritual resources, Ruth came to find life intolerable. Two years after coming to Wyoming, she gave birth to her tenth and final child, Miles Justus, her "sweet baby boy," on the night

---

* When Irma and Edith boarded in Burns to attend high school, they attended the local Presbyterian church.

Baby Miles Justus. *Author's collection.*

of Halley's Comet on May 18, 1910.[60] Almost immediately afterward, she began suffering from what twenty-first-century physicians would diagnose as post-partum depression.

Ruth's troubled mental state quickly manifested itself. Once, on a trip to Egbert, she was convinced that there were many people about, all waving to her. When she demanded an explanation from Edith, she was shocked to learn that there were no people at all. Her impaired vision could have partly accounted for this mistake, but there were similar episodes. Ruth became terrified that she was losing her mind.

The older children grew alarmed as well. Chester witnessed the situation first-hand during one of his visits home: "Mama felt that the end was near, and asked us older children to take care of her 'dear little boy'—Miles. I did not realize the seriousness of the whole situation—especially Mama's physical and mental situation, and the environmental conditions within which she had to carry the hard working responsibilities of caring for a large family."[61] Chester tried to broach the subject with his mother, but by then her condition was peaking to a crisis:

Now there was a real break—a nervous prostration seems to me to have been the trouble.

One evening she said to me, "Chester, do you think there is enough water in the creek so that I could drown myself?"

I did not fully realize her situation at the time. Papa was away from home; so was I building Sibley's phone line.

The first prayer that I ever uttered was one night after work, in a friend's non-used homestead shack. I prayed to a God whom I did not know for our mother's physical health and peace of mind.[62]

Miles, too, was deeply concerned about Ruth. On moving to Benton Harbor as a young man, he had found his grandmother Thebo in the Michigan Asylum for the Insane.[63] There she had remained for the last twenty-five years of her life, and there she had presumably died, just a few years earlier, in 1906. The memory of this tragedy was enough to propel Miles into action as he witnessed his wife's nervous collapse.

Porter Kellogg had by this time relocated to Southern California. After gathering in two consecutive poor harvests, Miles gratefully accepted his brother's offer of work in his residential construction business in San Diego. He worked there with Porter from January to April in both 1911 and 1912.[64] On the second of these trips, he took Ruth and baby Miles Justus with him, leaving the older children to look after themselves, their younger siblings and the homestead.

Ruth's trip west, which gave her the opportunity to visit with family and reap the restorative benefits of Southern California's balmy climate and cheery sunshine, was the perfect antidote for her fragile condition. When she returned home, it was obvious to the children that the extended vacation had done their mother a world of good, and from this point forward, she made a gradual recovery.

HOMESTEAD HIJINKS

As far as Miles and Ruth were concerned, life in Wyoming meant one nearly endless round of hardship. Not a day passed that they did not look ahead to the next with apprehension. Their children, however, took a different view. Neither hunger nor hard work could discourage them from reveling in the fun and adventure that accompanied homesteading on the wild prairies—a drastic switch from their former city life in Boulder.

Typical of most pioneer families, the Kelloggs kept a variety of farm animals, many of which also served as pets.* Vera and Helen each had a pet hen, named Ruth and Mildred, respectively, and Lloyd loved nothing better than saddling the family cow and riding it around the homestead. Also included in the family menagerie was a rafter of turkeys—animals that proved to be far more trouble than they were worth. None of the children could approach the birds except for tiny Dorothy, the only one who did not tease them. The turkeys allowed Dorothy to pet them and would lovingly follow her wherever she went, all the while aggressively pecking at her brothers and sisters to keep their distance.†

The most indispensable animal was Old Tom. In many ways, the Kelloggs' fate rested entirely with the thin, bony horse. It was Tom who

---

* The children also enjoyed playing with water snakes near Lodgepole Creek.

† The older children eventually had their revenge. When Christmas came around one year and a turkey was caught eating a pumpkin pie, the bird was promptly turned into the main dinner course.

pulled the family wagon, plowed the fields, shifted the cumbersome farming equipment and hauled the groceries from town. Adding to Tom's value were his many winning qualities, which endeared him to everyone in the family. He was observant, always noticing if something fell off his back or off the wagon behind him and, without any prompting, stopping for his passenger to climb down and retrieve it. Gentle by nature, he could also be trusted around the younger children. He grew so beloved that the Kelloggs came to regard him almost as a member of the family. When temperatures would drop dangerously low in the wintertime, Edith, Tom's primary caregiver, would stable him in her mother's pristine kitchen to ensure that he did not freeze to death in the barn. Miles, who perhaps appreciated the horse's value better than anyone, would never forget his faithful helper. Years later, while paying a visit to the old homestead, he composed "Memories of Old Horse Tom" in his honor:

> His stall is now empty, Old Tom he has gone,
>   No more will we feed him, noon, night and morn.
> So faithful and willing, so gentle and kind,
>   A whip never needed, he always would mind.
> And how we did miss him when to town we would go,
>   When the road was rough, he would go very slow.
> From town we'd ride home with a pack on his back;
>   If a parcel we'd drop, he would stop in his track.
>
> And the good Book says, in the world made new,
>   There will be lambs and lions. Why not Old Tom, too?

But the animals did not perform all of the work on the homestead. Every member of the family had chores to perform. Ruth taught her children the value of cleanliness by keeping the house in almost spotless condition. Each night, after Miles and the children were tucked up snuggly in bed, she would go through the house and pick up whatever they had left lying around so that everything would be tidy the next day. Sensitive as she was to her husband's criticism, she paid great attention to detail, even polishing the doorknobs. She also developed techniques to compensate for her poor eyesight, such as folding each child's clothing for the next day over his or her chair. The children grew so accustomed to their mother's fastidious ways that they were tempted to look down on friends and neighbors whose own standards did not come up to the same mark. One day, Murl revealed

Edith (*sixth from left*) and Irma (*second from right*) at high school in Burns. Edith's writing is on the blackboard. *Author's collection.*

his prejudices all too expressively when he caught his teacher sweeping dirt under the schoolhouse stove. Forthright to a fault, he informed her that she was not only "cracked" but "cracked all the way around."[65]

When Ruth fell ill, Edith took over the running of the household. Only eleven at the time of the move to Wyoming, she did all of the cooking, both at home and at her father's shop at Burns; she did all of the mending and sewing; and she served as a surrogate mother to her younger siblings. The small girl also acted as "man of the house" during her father's and older brother's frequent absences from home, performing the physically taxing chores of hauling the coal and taking care of Tom. Catching and saddling the horse by herself, she would ride him in all weathers—even blizzards—to pick up the family groceries from Burns.* The family ultimately dubbed Edith her mother's "right arm."[66]

Far from collapsing under such heavy burdens, Edith seemed to actually thrive on them. She not only was unfailingly cheerful and optimistic, but she also voluntarily added to her responsibilities by seeking work outside the home to augment the family's income. She would hire herself out to neighbors as a child-minder and housekeeper, and when deep snows prevented the regular teacher from reaching the schoolhouse, she would fill in as substitute.

---

* Sometimes staple foodstuffs like flour or sugar could be procured at a prearranged point along the railroad tracks that ran by the house. Whenever rations sank low, Miles would go out to meet the train and purchase barrels of flour and sacks of sugar by the hundred pound. More often than not, though, Miles was not at home, and provisions had to be procured in Burns.

Even the most mundane of Edith's activities could prove eventful, if not dangerous. Once, she accidently ran the needle of the family sewing machine through her finger. The needle remained stuck until a panicked Ruth managed to contact Chester in town via his homemade telephone to get his advice on how best to extract it. Another time, Edith was helping a neighbor woman with her children when the head of the house returned home drunk from the annual Cheyenne Frontier Days celebrations. Ordering his wife upstairs, the man seized his gun and told Edith to "scatter!" She instantly obeyed. Bolting out into the dark night and across the prairie, she never stopped running until she reached the safety of her own home. In the morning, the Kelloggs found the neighbor—still with his gun—fast asleep near their house.

Other times Edith was more congenially rewarded for her faithful service. Among her happiest memories was a glorious, once-in-a-lifetime experience that took place the night of her youngest brother's birth. Going out to milk the cow in the early morning hours, she was just in time to catch sight of the great Halley's Comet as it made its appearance for the first time in seventy-five years. To the end of her days, she would never forget the stunning sight the comet made as it filled the sky with its tail of many colors.

Edith, along with the rest of the family, also found the time to enjoy some much-needed recreation and relaxation. Making music together, the pastime that had played such a crucial role in Miles and Ruth's courtship, was by now part of the fabric of family life. In the evenings, everyone would gather around the organ to sing. Whenever Miles could be home in the summertime, the entire family would gather on the sod-top of the root cellar to lazily while away the time together.[*]

Christmas, too, remained as important as it had always been—especially to Miles. He made a point of being home for the holiday and continued his tradition of handcrafting a special gift for each of his many sons and daughters. One winter he arrived home from Burns looking like Santa Claus, toting a big bag of toys on his back. Sometimes there were even gifts of ready-made clothing, then a novelty, ordered from Sears & Roebuck mail-order catalogues. Every year Miles also insisted on a Christmas tree, no matter what kind was available. In Boulder, he had made an annual treat

---

[*] Chester described the cellar as a "10′x 12′structure set a few feet into the ground, extending three feet above the surface and walled up with stone." A sloping door served as its entrance. The roof, where the family gathered, was made of railroad ties covered with soil and sod.

The Kelloggs at a Fourth of July picnic in Egbert. *Author's collection.*

of taking the children up into the Rockies to select one. In Wyoming, the scarcity of traditional evergreens meant that they had to make do with one of the few scrubby trees that grew along the banks of nearby Lodgepole Creek. Bringing the tree home, they would trim it with traditional homemade decorations of cranberries, popcorn and paper chains.[*]

Most importantly of all, Christmas was a community event. The children would trudge a mile through the snow to sing Christmas carols at their teacher's house. Together with all the neighboring families, the Kelloggs would also attend an annual holiday program at the little schoolhouse. Miles was a regular speaker at this event, but one year, Dorothy, who was not even old enough yet to attend school, performed as well. Sitting up front in a little chair that her father had handcrafted just her size, she recited Margaret A. Richard's poem "The Child's Reason":

---

[*] Christmas dinner was yet another treat. Although the Kelloggs' diet usually followed the vegetarian guidelines of the Adventist health message, on Christmas Day, they feasted on turkey, Ruth's special dressing and mincemeat pie like other families.

She looked on the picture,
The wee little maid,
Of Christ, "the Good Shepherd,"
And softly she said,

"It's nicer to be
A lam' dan a s'eep!"
Then she blinked her blue eyes,
As though near asleep.

"But why, precious one?"
'Twas the hour of rest,
And the mother held close
Her child to her breast.

"Tause Desus," she answered,
In babyish talk,
"Takes de lam' in his arms,
But de s'eeps has to walk!" [67]

Adding further interest to life was the wide variety of unsupervised and highly unconventional hobbies that the children dreamed up for themselves. Although they had some playthings—Miles built a merry-go-round and Chester a large swing from discarded telephone poles—the relative dearth of modern, sophisticated toys meant that the children had to fall back on their native ingenuity—an inheritance from their father—to create their own fun. This necessity, coupled with a family penchant for pranks, ensured that life on the prairies was never dull.

The younger children were especially adept at harnessing their surroundings for their amusement. They would spend hours outside after every snowfall playing one of their favorite games—"flying to the clouds." Climbing to the top of the snow-covered house, they would "fly" down to the snow below. Murl and Lloyd especially loved the game. Flapping his arms vigorously, Murl would cry out enthusiastically, "Clouds, I'll be up there in a minute!"[68] Lloyd, meanwhile, would arm himself with an open parasol for his "flight"—only for the parasol to turn inside out on his way down.

But the older children—most notably, Chester—found ways to unleash their creativity as well. The teenaged Chester had by this time developed a keen, albeit questionable, sense of humor. He was fascinated by electricity,

Above: Vida Hall, the Kellogg children's beloved teacher. *Author's collection.*

Left: Miles Justus, aged two, and Dorothy, aged four. *Author's collection.*

Irma and Edith with Vida Hall and other friends. Back row: Irma (*second from left*). Front row: Vida (*left*) and Edith (*dressed in all white*). *Author's collection.*

the harnessing of which in the early 1900s still seemed to offer endlessly novel and exciting possibilities, and he never missed an opportunity to conduct an experiment. Once, he placed some pennies in a pan of water and electrified it. Eager to observe a reaction, he tried (unsuccessfully) to persuade Edith to participate in his experiment by telling her that she could have the coins if she could get them. Chester's most notorious prank, however, was one that he pulled on his father. Edith recounted the story:

> *Papa and Chester…were not always away from home. Chester was there long enough to set up a phone from* [our] *home to that of a neighbor who lived nearer town. Of course, all the gates had to be closed, for the phone used the fence wire to carry the messages. The phone had to be cranked to generate the necessary electricity, and one day Chester thought it would be great sport to electrify the seat of the outhouse. He ran a wire from the crank generator of the phone to the outhouse—a thin black wire, not*

easy to see. It just happened that [our] father was sick, and had to rush frequently to that little outhouse. He was in such a hurry he did not notice that little black wire. Chester talked [our] little sister Dorothy into giving the crank a vigorous tug at just the right moment. There was an immediate reaction! [69] *

Further excitement came from a couple of "wandering" adventures. One day, Irma was walking from Egbert to Burns when she became disoriented, likely due to exhaustion. Spying a house along her route, she entered it without invitation and, much to the amazement of its owner, promptly went to sleep.

Helen was the center of an even more incredible episode—an almost unbelievable case of nocturnal sleepwalking that took place not long after the move to Wyoming. Chester related what happened that summer's night:

On one evening, when the story hour was over, we separated for our night quarters. Soon after, Mama was making rounds to our bedrooms in search for Helen.

Helen was approximately six years of age. She was dressed in light gingham and was barefoot. She was not to be found around the home, the poultry house, or the barn.

I mounted the horse and rode about the gardens. Here I met the familiar buzz of a rattler. Tom shied off. Next I followed along the creek; another rattler!

Papa requested me to call out some of the neighbors; so Hobbses, Burrows, and Purinlam with his collie, entered the search over the hills and meadows. Papa, with a lantern, went north along the section-line fence. Less than a mile to the northwest, lived Dan Brewer. There Papa found Helen.

Dan had left the kitchen door and headed for the corral but stopped short. There was something moving among the cattle. Not being able to distinguish it in the darkness, he took it for a coyote. Slipping back to the door, he called, "Dot, hand me the rifle."

"O, Dan, what for?"

"Something among the cattle."

"Let me see," Dot loudly whispered.

"Give me that rifle," excitedly demanded Dan.

But Dot had to see for herself. Scarcely had Dan uttered his last words, when Dot was slipping through the gate bars. Cautiously moving among the

---

* "You would do that to your old father, would you?" Miles demanded before he whipped Chester.

81

herd toward where she thought she had seen just two legs of something, Dot came right up to "it."

Yes, it was our little sister Helen. Cuddling the now-awake little girl, the three were soon in the house. Helen was recognized as one of the little Kellogg girls. Almost simultaneously with their finding Helen, Papa was entering the Brewer yard, thinking that perhaps....

Helen had, evidently, left the story-telling hour asleep; walked a hundred feet to the line fence of four barbed-wire strands; crawled through without tearing her dress; bare-footed it through the prairie grass and around clumps of prickly pear cactus; and, perhaps seeing the Brewers' house lights in the distance, went on, still asleep, through another wire fence; and through the rail fence of the corral. Not a tear in her clothing or a scratch on her feet.

Papa brought her home, pick-a-back, waving his lantern to other searchers as a signal of success. There was rejoicing at home, that summer night.[70]

A PORT OF SALVATION

Ruth's transformed appearance on her return home from San Diego was a herald of better things to come. The next several months flew by as the family prepared to leave homesteading behind and begin a new life in California. While Ruth boarded the train back to the homestead in the early months of 1912,[71] Miles lingered temporarily in California, sending for Chester to join him. Father and son worked together for Porter until Miles's return to Wyoming at the end of April.[72] Around August, Miles, not yet entirely convinced about his ability to provide for his large family in San Diego, made a trip back to Minnesota to explore its employment opportunities. Taking his wife and baby Miles Justus with him so that Ruth could enjoy a much-longed-for reunion with her parents, brothers and extended family, he left Edith in charge of the other children and the homestead for three months.[73] When the grown-ups returned to Wyoming that fall, Chester sent train fare for Irma and Vera so that they could join him in San Diego. Together, the three of them prepared the house that Chester had started renting for the arrival of their mother and the other children in early February of the next year.

Miles's own movements for the next several months remain a mystery. Official homestead records make it clear that he, along with the rest of the family, left Wyoming at the earliest possible moment. January 28, 1913, marked the five-year anniversary of the Kelloggs' residence on the homestead,[74] at which point the 160 acres became Miles's undisputed legal property. Less than a week later, the entire family—Miles included—

moved off the homestead.[75] But while Ruth and the children moved in with Chester in San Diego, there is no written or oral record to account for Miles's whereabouts.

The only clue to his activities comes from his oldest son's memoirs. For unknown reasons, Chester had parted company with his uncle Porter shortly after his father's departure from California and "was soon on [his] own initiative and responsibility."[76] Now the temporary head and breadwinner of the family, Chester "had regular employment and was, therefore, able to support the family."[77] This suggests that his middle-aged father and uncle, despite their superior experience, might have encountered more difficulty than a strapping twenty-year-old in finding employment during the mini-depressions that occasionally struck San Diego and put carpenters out of work.

It fell to Chester to support the entire family, for several months, on his "journeyman's wages—four dollars for eight hours."[78] The pressures of this responsibility weighed heavily on the young man's shoulders, but even then, the professional manner that he had learned from his father stood him in good stead, helping him to secure a steady job:

> I walked the city day by day, seeking employment. I do recall one very encouraging experience. Walking energetically onto a building project, I inquired of the foreman, "Sir, can you use another man?"
>
> His curt reply, "No!"
>
> With a "Thank you, sir," I turned upon my heel and made for the street. I needed employment; there was no time to be wasted in loitering around. Before I had reached the sidewalk, I was really startled by, "Hey, come back here."
>
> It was the same voice that had uttered that curt "No" to my inquiry. It added, "Come back Monday." I was there. And I was still there on those projects of Kirby and Carnahan until the early fall of 1913, when I departed for San Fernando.
>
> On one occasion, when I had called at the downtown office for my check, Mr. Kirby paid me a real compliment. Said he, "You know, Kellogg, Joe tells me that he never saw a carpenter turn out so much work as you do." It was not so much hard work and fast action as it was short cuts in procedure that made the accomplishment possible.
>
> At about this same time Joe Carnahan observed, "Chester, do you know why I changed my mind and hired you that day when you came on the Job? You came like you meant business; and what was more, you left

in the same way. I needed help like that." The facts were that both these compliments belonged to our father. He seems to have gotten the ideas into all of his boys.[79]

It was also during this time that Chester joined the Seventh-day Adventist Church. When he had first arrived in San Diego, his aunt Mary (Porter's second wife) had urged him to attend a series of tent meetings that was then being held on San Diego's University Avenue. Chester, whose childhood memories of Adventism were fairly dim by this time, soon began attending night after night. Only a little younger than Miles had been when he had first attended the Benton Harbor meetings, Chester listened to the evangelists' messages with attention just as rapt as his father's had been.

Through Chester's influence, Adventism gradually came to define the family's way of life once more. Ruth rejoined the Adventist Church not long after her arrival in San Diego—a decision that was no doubt made easier by her husband's absence. Her example would have a far-reaching significance for her many sons and daughters, most of whom had no recollection of their parents' previous affiliation with Adventism. All but one would eventually make the decision to be baptized into the Adventist Church.*

Ruth and the children had become firmly entrenched in the local Adventist community by the time Miles resumed their support in mid-1913. The first thing he did was to remove them from the house that Chester had been renting from W.M. Healey, an Adventist elder and the founder of the local Adventist school, and install them in another rental property situated directly across the street from a firehouse.† Several months later, Miles found the means to build a house for them in National City, located between San Diego and Chula Vista.

The move to National City coincided with the breaking up of the family as, one by one, the older children began to leave home. Irma, who had never gotten along with her father at the best of times, found a new home in an apartment house owned by a family friend from Wyoming. Edith

---

* Other aspects of the children's reassimilation into civilization were not so easily accomplished. Porter's children regarded their Wyoming cousins as little more than country bumpkins and played tricks on them by way of a welcome. They also disdained their "country cousins'" ignorance of what they considered to be general knowledge. It was an uncomfortable moment when Vera, almost a teenager, piped up in Sabbath School to ask the teacher, in all innocence, to explain circumcision. The teacher, embarrassed, refused to answer and instead referred Vera to another girl for information.

† The house's location was a source of endless delight for the younger children. They loved gazing at the horses inside the firehouse, and they would stare in fascination when the harnesses dropped onto the horses upon the ringing of the fire bell.

Porter Kellogg's son Arthur *(far left)* and daughter Ethel *(far right)* with friends by the sea. *Author's collection.*

and Vera quickly followed suit, going to work full-time in San Diego's fish canneries and boarding in town with a housepainter named Thomas Wright and his wife, Lola.*

But it was Chester's leave-taking that brought about the most dramatic change. Miles, perhaps due to his own limited formal schooling, had not placed a high value on education, at least where his oldest son was concerned. Whenever he had needed an extra pair of hands at work in Boulder, he had not hesitated to pull Chester out of school. In Wyoming, he had expected Chester to go to work full-time to help ensure the family's survival—an expectation to which Chester had selflessly bowed. All the same, Chester had continued to cherish hopes of a life beyond basic trade skills and hand-to-mouth wages—hopes to which his father, with his inverted snobbery and preoccupation with providing food and clothing for his large family, remained decidedly unsympathetic. Chester later remarked, "I think…that I felt above the grade-level to which I was bound. I was living in the electrical engineering world, and my reading led me into that field of reading. I recall asking Papa to pay for a course of study with the International Correspondence School in Scranton, Pa. His

* Ruth somehow found the means to regularly send ticket fare to the girls so that they could come home on the weekends to spend Sabbath with the rest of the family.

reply: 'Finish eight grades of schoolwork, then you will be on your own.' Well, that was it.'"[80]

Chester had not been one to wallow in self-pity, however. Shouldering his burden cheerfully, he had taken advantage of the few opportunities for self-improvement that had been available in Wyoming, participating in a literary society and a debating team and attending prayer meetings at a local church. By the time he moved to San Diego, a college education had become a fixed goal in his mind, and he had begun planning accordingly, seizing every chance for overtime work and setting aside the extra wages for his education fund. Even after financing his mother's and siblings' train fare west, he was able to save a total of $100. As further preparation, he put himself through a course of self-directed study, teaching himself business arithmetic and high school freshman English as he rode the streetcars to and from work each day.

By the early fall of 1913, Chester was ready to take his future in hand. His father's inevitable objections notwithstanding, the twenty-one-year-old packed his clothing, bedding and books into a "little round-top family trunk" and set off for San Fernando, a little town north of Los Angeles, where he enrolled in the Adventist academy.[81]

Those left at home immediately felt the effects of Chester's departure. In the absence of his wages, the younger children—especially the boys—now had to do their share to put food on the table. Murl found work digging ditches, and Lloyd, accompanied by little Miles Justus, drove a horse-drawn grocery delivery wagon to the Adventists' Paradise Valley Sanitarium. Yet the boys' earnings could not offset their older brother's more substantial contributions. At one point, funds sank so low that Chester had to temporarily suspend his studies in San Fernando and resume working full-time so that the family could afford to purchase basic necessities.

Rendering the financial situation all the more acute was a dwindling local demand for carpentry work. This compelled Miles to turn his ever-innovative mind to coming up with new and unique ways of earning an income.* His most notable venture during this time was a special health food product, inspired by his family's renewed association with the health-conscious Adventists. With the help of Edith and Vera's landlord, Thomas Wright,† he developed carrot butter, or "carobutter" as he called it, from a recipe of carrots and sweet potatoes. He and Thomas packaged the carobutter like

---

* Miles, concluding that San Diego proper offered the best work prospects, ended up living apart from his family, much as he had in Wyoming. He would return home once a week to supply Ruth and the children with fresh fruit every Monday.

† One of the younger Kellogg children asserted that it was Thomas's teenaged son, Vinton—not Thomas himself—who assisted Miles in the carobutter enterprise.

regular dairy butter, leaving it to set in handmade, butter-shaped molds and afterward wrapping it in paper. The two men launched a small campaign in San Fernando, and the carobutter enjoyed promising early sales. But this success was short-lived. Miles and Thomas had to discontinue the carobutter after only a few months, when customers began to complain that it spoiled after two or three days.

It was not solely economic failures, however, that ultimately prompted Miles to move his family from San Diego. In January 1916, heavy rains caused widespread flooding. The disaster took a devastating toll throughout San Diego County, resulting in tragic losses of both life and property. The Kelloggs were more fortunate than most. Miles, as if foreseeing the flood, had built his house on stilts. Although he had to travel by boat to reach it, the rest of the family was kept literally high and dry until the waters receded.

Members of the family responded to the disaster with mixed reactions. To the youngest children, the flood was nothing short of an adventure. Standing

Miles's uncle, George Thebo. *Author's collection.*

Encinitas (looking west toward the ocean) as the Kelloggs first knew it in the 1910s. The Hammond Hotel, its top story intact, is at left. *Author's collection.*

at the corner of the property fence, Lloyd, Dorothy and Miles Justus would reach out to catch oranges or whatever else they spied floating by and would watch in awe as horses were swept away by the flow.

To Miles, on the other hand, the flood was the last straw. About a year earlier, he had abandoned the idea of ever securing permanent work in San Diego. Porter had moved back to Boulder after his house in San Diego's Encanto neighborhood had burned down, leaving Miles without a business partner.

With few other options in sight, Miles had once again turned to relatives to determine his next step. Two of his mother's younger brothers, George Thebo and Jess Thebo, had also come west and had settled in the sleepy little coastal town of Encinitas, just twenty-five miles north of San Diego. Known for their heavy drinking, tobacco spitting and strong language, the Thebo brothers led lifestyles that were starkly at odds with Miles's own, but by this time he had nowhere else to turn. He gratefully accepted his uncle Jess's offer of employment doing unskilled labor. Jess, who was just a couple of years older than Miles, ran a business harvesting rock and kelp off the coast. A kelp catcher from San Diego would run along the coast of Encinitas's Moonlight Beach and collect kelp. It was Miles's job to gather any kelp that the barges missed, load it into wagons and transport it to the train station to be sent down to San Diego.*

In the summer of 1916, Miles arranged for Ruth and the children to join him in Encinitas. With his mind squarely centered on simply earning enough money to feed and clothe his family, he little suspected the tremendous effect that this decision would have on his future. It was in Encinitas that he and Ruth would make their home for over fifteen years—the longest residence of their married life—and that he would enjoy the greatest financial prosperity that he had ever known. Most importantly, it was there that he would achieve an enduring reputation as one of San Diego County's most innovative architects.

---

* In this way, Miles, who likely still held the pacifist views espoused by Seventh-day Adventists, contributed to the war effort. The outbreak of the First World War in 1914 and the United States' entrance into the international fray three years later generated a demand for substances derived from kelp, such as iodine. Iodine deficiency was responsible for exempting many otherwise physically fit young men from selective service. Kelp also played an important role in the manufacturing of explosives.

HIGH TIMES AT THE HAMMOND HOTEL

G rateful though he was for a chance to support his family, Miles was not destined to stay in the backbreaking work of kelp harvesting for long. Now in his mid-forties, he was accustomed to being his own master and having an outlet for his creativity. It was only a matter of time before his fortunes changed, and he began securing steady building work once more.

Encinitas, as it turned out, was in great need of experienced builders, and Miles was just the man to fill this need. Not long after he moved his family up from San Diego, the *Oceanside Blade* published a glowing testimonial of his skills:

> *Building Is Active around Encinitas*
> *Contractor Kellogg Erects Three Nice Houses*
> *for Prosperous Ranchers of That Section*

> *M.M. Kellogg, general contractor of Encinitas, has been busy recently with a number of improvements in the building line in and around Encinitas. Mr. Kellogg this week completed a neat house and large barn for George Ward who has leased a portion of the Kelly ranch and will raise beans. A gas engine and domestic water system are among the conveniences he has installed on the property which he is putting into fine shape.*

> *Another of the contracts completed recently by Mr. Kellogg is a fine seven room modern house for F.L. Scott on the Jones ranch in Green valley*

which was recently purchased by Mr. Scott. The ranch contains 110 acres, seventy acres of which are in bean, besides an orchard. The house is built around a court sixteen by thirteen feet in extent and there are large porches on three sides. The new home is wired for electricity and is equipped with an acetylene gas plant. Lawns and cement walks are being put in and in a short time Mr. Scott will have one of the handsomest homes in the entire section.

Next week Mr. Kellogg will be busy with a five room plastered bungalow which he will build for J.N. Thilges on his property three miles northeast of Encinitas. The new house will be modern in every respect. A large cement reservoir and pumping system will furnish water for domestic use. Mr. Thilges is one of the successful farmers of the Encinitas country. He has engaged in bean raising and has found the occupation so profitable that he has paid for his ranch in the three years since its purchase besides providing for the building of his new home.[82]

As the year 1917 gave way to 1918, Miles found himself prosperous enough to purchase the town's historic Hammond Hotel.[*] Built around the 1880s by E.G. Hammond,[†] one of Encinitas's founding fathers, the commodious, three-story building dated to Southern California's stagecoach days. Original hitching posts and a large green bell stood beside it to mark the old stagecoach line—the historic El Camino Real, which became Highway 101. The hotel was ideally situated in Encinitas. Adjacent to both the railroad tracks and the commercial building that housed Miles's carpenter's and blacksmith's shops, it was also just down the road from the post office and his uncle George's restaurant.

But Miles did not purchase the Hammond Hotel to run it exclusively as lodging for paying guests.[‡] Renting out only the third floor to agricultural workers, he devoted the second to living quarters for his family[§] and the first to accommodating the various side businesses that he ran to supplement his building income. These enterprises included manufacturing beehives and numerous small bean cleaners for the local Hutching Bros[83] and running a shoe shop, a hardware store (from which he installed the first "light plants"

---

[*] It was also known as the "Pitcher House" or the "old Encinitas Hotel."

[†] Miles's uncle George Thebo was among the local men who had helped in the construction.

[‡] When Miles had first arrived in Encinitas, he had boarded with his uncle George and aunt Emmy Thebo. After Ruth and the children had joined him, he had rented a house near the ocean.

[§] At a time when Encinitas had no running water, Miles gave his family this luxury by digging a well and building a cistern with a water tower tall enough to reach the second floor.

The Hammond Hotel, circa 1900. The hotel had an updated, square porch when the Kelloggs moved in during the 1910s. *Encinitas Historical Society.*

in town)[84] and (after his commercial building next door burned down) his carpenter's and blacksmith's shops.*

Miles also manufactured food products on the hotel property. Using a self-made sorghum press, he made molasses from both sorghum and sugar cane. The *Oceanside Blade* reported in September 1918: "Miles Kellogg, who believes in trying out many things and usually makes a success of them, has been experimenting with the making of sorghum syrup. He has turned out a very good product, most of it having been sold to autoists going by and next season expects to manufacture it on a larger scale."[85]

With fruit from an orchard in nearby Spring Valley, Miles turned out hard apple cider by the fifty-gallon drum until Prohibition took effect in 1920. Miles, clearly disgruntled at having to give up what was possibly one of his more lucrative ventures, outlined his own proposed alternative to Prohibition:

---

* With the daylight hours devoted primarily to building projects, Miles ran the shoe shop at night and spent the early morning hours making beehive boxes. Although he sold some of these boxes, he kept a few for himself. He worked two or three beehives a year.

Take away all profit in it [the manufacturing of alcohol] *by letting anyone make it as cheap as lemonade, and we would have no bootlegging or hijacking. And all the crime and murders over the profits. Also a big decrease in taxes.*

Substitute for the 18ᵗʰ Amendment strict laws punishing severely anyone abusing the use of it. To wit, one should not be allowed in any public place with even the smell of it on him, as the line cannot be drawn that establishes the point of sobriety and drunkenness. And especially this should apply to one driving an auto.[86]

His children's contributions helped ensure the family's continued financial solvency. When the Kelloggs first arrived in Encinitas, everyone—even Miles Justus, then only five or six years old—had joined Miles in picking kelp off the coast. Now, from the oldest to the youngest, everyone still living at home continued to earn their keep. Each of the boys helped run at least one of their father's enterprises, working for him every day after school, on Sundays and during vacations. Murl worked in Miles's construction business, Lloyd helped make the beehive boxes and grade-school-aged Miles Justus did his share by stacking lumber behind the hotel every afternoon after school and helping his father paint a little schoolhouse in nearby Green Valley.

The girls worked just as hard. Giving up their jobs at the San Diego fish canneries, Edith and Vera rejoined the family in Encinitas. Vera's first job was at George Thebo's restaurant, but soon both teenaged girls were hiring themselves out as child-minders and housekeepers to local residents.* They earned additional money at harvest time by cleaning lima beans at a local farm, where they became known as the cleanest and fastest workers. Eight-year-old Dorothy joined her older sisters during the harvests, earning her first money, like other local little girls, by picking up beans after the thresher went by.

Ruth, meanwhile, continued to run a tight ship at home. Even with her poor eyesight, she was able to maintain her usual high standards of housekeeping by relying on her other senses. (She would check Dorothy's work after every sweeping by removing her shoes and feeling the floor with her bare feet.) As for the household tasks that Ruth could not supervise, such as the sewing, the family found ways to improvise: Miles ended up purchasing much of the family's clothing after Edith, the family seamstress, left home permanently.†

---

* One of Edith's employers was the Ginn family in Del Mar. A member of the well-known family of New York textbook publishers, Maurice Edwin Ginn hired Edith to take care of his small children.

† This arrangement met with questionable success because Miles invariably purchased every article of clothing in his favorite color, blue.

George Thebo outside his restaurant. *Author's collection.*

Nevertheless, life was not all work and no play. Miles, despite being a stern taskmaster, ensured that his children had time for fun and recreation.* Christmas remained a much-cherished family holiday. Every Christmas morning, the children would enter the hotel's dining room to find the enormous table festively decorated. There would be a special place set for each of them garnished with fruit, some of Ruth's homemade candy and a small gift.

Another source of fun was the assortment of pets that the children were allowed to keep. Everyone in the family, including Miles and Ruth, loved

---

* Miles made one exception to his children's leisure activities. Concerned that they would permanently injure themselves, he would not allow his sons to play football.

Edith (*second from left*) with friends and one of her charges. Standing beside her is Encinitas local boy Johnny Reseck. *Author's collection.*

animals,* and at various times, the Kelloggs owned cats, dogs and guinea pigs. Whenever one of these beloved creatures died—several perished on the railroad tracks that ran beside the hotel—it was given a tender burial in the family's pet cemetery in the backyard.

Even more entertaining was the veritable zoo that some family friends, the Coutts, kept at their ranch. Fred Coutts, an animal trainer who would go on to befriend singer Bing Crosby, had as pets a monkey, a skunk that had undergone an operation to rid it of its stink and a raccoon that lived indoors with the family.†

The First World War also presented new and exciting opportunities, at least for the girls. The Kelloggs, along with other local Christian families, made it a mission to host parties at their own home so that the soldiers from the nearby camp could have a wholesome alternative to dance halls. Predictably, many of the soldiers, knowing that they would soon be shipped overseas, became attracted to the older Kellogg girls. Observing this, the younger girls, anxious for a share in the attention, went out of their way to seek the soldiers out at their camp. Lloyd, Dorothy and Miles Justus were

---

* Miles allegedly once built a small door into the barn for the family cat. On discovering that its kittens were unable to pass through the door, he thoughtfully built another one, just their size, through which they could follow their mother in and out of the barn.

† One day, the Coutts family returned home to find their bathroom flooded. The raccoon had had fun with the water taps in the bathtub and had allowed it to overflow.

Right: Irma outside the Paradise Valley Sanitarium. *Author's collection.*

Below: On the porch of the Hammond Hotel. Back row: Miles, Professor Hall (principal of San Fernando Academy), Vera, Dorothy. Front row: Ruth, Irma, Edith. *Author's collection.*

already in the habit of borrowing their friend Kathryn Cozens's* pony and hitching it to a wagon to drive around Encinitas. Now Lloyd painted a red cross on the back of the wagon, and Dorothy and her friend Irene Rupe, dressed as Red Cross nurses, would drive to where the soldiers were camped by the bluffs.†

Too young for conscription, the Kellogg boys were far more interested in machinery than in befriending the soldiers. They spent almost all of their free time with cars and motorcycles. Perhaps in partial compensation for their faithful, hard work (he did not pay them wages until they married), Miles allowed his sons to have their own cars, on the condition that the vehicles did not break down and have to go to the garage.‡

Even Miles found time for a few leisure pursuits, such as making music and scribbling verses. Every so often he would take a break from work and go upstairs to the family parlor on the hotel's second floor to spend an hour or two playing the piano and singing. He also resumed poetry writing. Miles produced one poem in the fall of 1918, just days after word reached his neighbor Peter Lux that his son Jesse had been killed in action in France. Jesse, born and raised in Encinitas, was a farmer and, as such, could have sought exemption from the draft. However, he had gone voluntarily. Jesse was the first local boy to die in the war.[87] Published in the *Oceanside Blade*, Miles's poem was dedicated to Jesse's memory:

In Memory of Jesse Lux

To day we feel sadly,
  And our hearts are wrung
For a friend and neighbor,
  Who has lost a son.

On the field of battle
  His all, his life he gave,
And in a foreign country
  There's another nameless grave.

---

* Kathryn was a granddaughter of pioneer settler E.G. Hammond.

† Ruth also unintentionally found herself caught up in a romance. Taking a motherly interest in the soldiers shipped overseas to Europe, she wrote to one, only for him to respond with a photograph and love letters. She had to tell him that she was married and had children.

‡ Miles apparently never had the heart to make good on his threat of confiscating the cars if anything went wrong. The boys were allowed to keep their unreliable, secondhand jalopies even when they had to spend time at Warner Rathyen's Midnite Garage.

But God, in His great mercy,
  Who notes the sparrow's fall,
Will not o'erlook that grave
  At the last great trumpet's call.

For he was true and noble,
  Yes, both generous and brave,
Who, for the cause of freedom,
  His all, his life he gave.
    M.M.K.[88]

It was Miles's inventing, however, that garnered the most attention. Throughout his years in Encinitas, he regularly impressed his neighbors and charmed his children with his innovative projects. Not all of his inventions were successes—a croquet set made from bamboo did not last long because the wood split on impact*—but many were, including two practical gadgets: a "gang" drill that cut four holes in the beehive boxes with one motion of the foot and a paintbrush that held paint in such a way that the brush did not have to be manually dipped into the paint. He also developed a new hatchet based on the one that he had designed in Boulder.

One of his most popular inventions was the Ride through the Clouds, a makeshift amusement park ride that was undoubtedly inspired by his visit to the Panama-California exposition in San Diego in 1915 or 1916. It consisted of a basket—large enough to fit one small child at a time—suspended on a rope, which he rigged up on a pulley at the top of the Hammond Hotel. The older children would pull the younger ones up, one by one, "to the clouds," before letting the basket slide back down to earth. Predictably, the contraption drew every child in town to the hotel.

Even more remarkable than the Ride through the Clouds, however, was the "invention" that Miles created many years after moving to Encinitas. Destined to become his most famous accomplishment, as well as his adopted hometown's most popular tourist attraction, it consisted of two pieces of highly innovative architecture, the likes of which few people had ever seen.

---

* Miles also made a croquet set from locally grown eucalyptus that was showcased as part of the Encinitas Farm Bureau's exhibit at the San Diego Fair in 1920. "Encinitas," *Blade Tribune*, October 2, 1920.

10
KELLOGG AND SONS

Despite the energy that Miles poured into his multifarious business ventures, building remained his primary source of income. The timing of his move to Encinitas had been auspicious. During the 1920s, Encinitas experienced an unprecedented growth in population, which in turn boosted local demand for construction work. Before long, what had been a tiny coastal village burgeoned into a small city that would be frequented by Hollywood stars such as Charles Chaplin, Bessie Love and Bing Crosby.

To meet demand, Miles and Murl founded a construction company, Kellogg & Son. The company's earliest commissions tended to be for agricultural buildings: In 1919, Miles built the packing house on Cozens & Son's ranch in Green Valley[89] and in 1922, a garage for Henry Lux to store his honey materials.[90] But Kellogg & Son ultimately specialized in houses, erecting many, if not most, of the new residential buildings that emerged throughout Encinitas and the outlying communities of Cardiff, Leucadia, South Coast Park and Green Valley. For years to come, these Kellogg houses would be recognizable by their signature "old Spanish," or frame stucco design, a style that other local builders would imitate.*

In addition, Kellogg & Son erected commercial buildings, such as grocery stores and pool halls. In 1924, Miles built a stucco strip mall onto the back of the Hammond Hotel. Known as the "Kellogg building,"[91] it

---

* The composer Bernard Hamblen rented a house built by Kellogg & Son.

A typical "Kellogg special." *Author's collection.*

faced Highway 101 and housed the popular Al's Barbershop,* the building and loan office and the office for the local newspaper, the *Coast-Dispatch*. The strip mall's official opening took place in January of the following year. The *Oceanside Blade* informed the public: "The new Encinitas branch of the Southwest Union Securities Corporation and the Community Building and Loan Association was formally opened Monday. These corporations are located in a building especially constructed for them by M.M. Kellogg and located on the main business street of Encinitas. The offices are 20x30 feet in dimensions, handsomely furnished and fitted up as modern banking quarters."[92]

Through his construction work, Miles became a prominent real estate holder. Whenever he was not building for clients, he would build rental houses and other properties for himself throughout the South Coast. At one point, he was leasing as many as twenty rentals within just two blocks. By 1925, he was regarded as "one of Encinitas' most substantial citizens" and had acquired an estimated $30,000 worth of property.[93†]

Miles further augmented his income by establishing the first lumberyard that Encinitas had had for many years.‡ There was more than a little irony in the meaning of Encinitas's name—"little oaks," which suggests an

---

* The barbershop had previously been housed in one of the Hammond Hotel's rental spaces.

† According to various online inflation calculators, this was the equivalent of nearly $450,000 in early 2020.

‡ The public-spirited Miles lent lumber from his yard to serve as tables at the annual meeting of the Encinitas Farm Bureau in 1922. "Encinitas," *Blade Tribune*, November 18, 1922.

abundance or, at least, a noticeable presence of indigenous trees. Aside from the namesake scrub oaks, native lumber had always been in notoriously short supply, and before Miles founded the Encinitas Lumber Company behind the Hammond Hotel, anyone wishing to build in the area had to have lumber specially shipped up from San Diego. In the fall of 1916, the following advertisement appeared in the *Oceanside Blade*:

> *The Encinitas Lumber Yard*
> *Just Arrived in Encinitas—a Young Lumber Yard*
> *Although young it is fully developed and can furnish all material for an ordinary house or barn.*
> *Standards goods; San Diego Prices*
> *Will make a specialty of cheap materials for repair work and small buildings, as well as the best qualities. Also Prepared Roofing, Chimney Tile, etc.*
> *M.M. Kellogg, Proprietor*
> *Also General Contractor*[94]

In January 1920, Miles installed "a new ten-horsepower electric motor in his shop which [would] take the place of the three gas engines now used for pumping, grinding and planing."[95] The next year he built a new planing mill, measuring twenty-four by sixty-four feet, for the purposes of manufacturing

The "Kellogg building" strip mall along Highway 101. Left to right: the *Coast-Dispatch* office, building and loan office, Al's Barbershop, converted Hammond Hotel. *Author's collection.*

his own line of furniture.[96] This planing mill also powered Miles's gristmill, which he had purchased in late 1917[97] to grind wheat and corn. Farmers would come to the lumberyard to have their wheat ground into flour, paying Miles for the use of the mill with half the resulting flour. Miles would then trade the flour to other townspeople to meet certain expenses, such as the cost of the music lessons Dorothy took from local piano teacher Gertrude Hammond Lauer,[98] or sell to the Paradise Valley Sanitarium or the Adventist-run vegetarian café in San Diego.[99] (Not everyone in Encinitas was pleased with the gristmill. It was so loud that Miles's neighbor Peter Lux complained until Miles put a muffler over the engine to deaden the noise.) Miles ran the lumberyard until 1924, when he sold it to the Solana Beach Lumber Company.[100]*

Miles might have achieved even greater success if he had had all four of his sons working for him. After establishing himself in Encinitas, he had undoubtedly cherished hopes that, one by one, Chester, Murl, Lloyd and Miles Justus would all join him as business partners. He could have then expected to see Kellogg & Son thrive and expand until it cornered part of the South Coast's ever-growing construction market. But such hopes were crushed early on, and for this Miles had only himself—and his temper—to blame.

Much to his delight, Chester had returned to San Diego with his new bride, Clara, in the summer of 1916, just in time to accompany the rest of the family to Encinitas. At first, the renewed father-and-son collaboration had gone smoothly. However, before many months had passed, Miles's ever-volatile temper had gotten the best of him—and lost him his oldest son's professional assistance forever.

He and Chester had been building a house on a ranch outside of town for a certain F.L. Scott, from whom Chester and Clara also happened to be renting a cottage. Scott, as it happened, owed Miles money and was not forthcoming with repayment. Consequently, Miles was appalled—and presumably felt betrayed—when he learned that Chester, obeying the dictates of his conscience, was continuing to pay rent to the defaulting rancher. When Chester refused to alter his course of action, an infuriated Miles lashed out at his son, "If you can't get along, move along. Go and be d—d!"[101]

Miles almost immediately regretted his harsh words, and his remorse deepened when Chester fell gravely ill with influenza shortly afterward. Chester knew his father well enough to interpret his anxious vigil by

---

* After so many years of working with wood, Miles was so expert that he could accurately estimate the amount of lumber in a tree simply by looking at it.

Left: Ruth in her husband's lumberyard. *Author's collection.*

Right: Chester (*left*) and Murl. *Author's collection.*

his sickbed as a tacit apology, but Miles, never known to apologize for anything in his life, did not openly express regret. Chester, accordingly, took his father at his word. As soon as he recovered, he and Clara left Encinitas for her family's home in Imperial Valley. They never returned to Encinitas except to pay brief visits, and Chester went on to pursue a career in Adventist education.

Instead of learning from this dismal lesson, Miles repeated the same mistake a few years later with Lloyd. Lloyd, the most mischievous of the Kellogg boys, continually tested his father's patience by sneaking off to shoot pool, getting drunk on Miles's homemade cider, selling moonshine for bootleggers* and dragging home countless stray animals. In this last activity, at least, Lloyd found some common ground with his father, who

---

* Assisting Lloyd in his business venture was his best friend, Waldo Lauer, a grandson of pioneer settler E.G. Hammond.

loved animals almost as much as he did. Once, when he brought home a dog from the dump—a locale that Miles had expressly forbidden his son from exploring—Miles, rather than refusing outright to let Lloyd keep his new pet, issued an ultimatum: Either Lloyd took a whipping as punishment, or he had to give up the dog. Lloyd chose the whipping, and the dog, whom he named Prince, became beloved by the entire family. Miles, usually stoically restrained in expressing his more tender emotions, actually wept when Prince died.

But Miles did not sympathize with Lloyd's greatest passion—motors. With the advent of the "horseless carriage" and the Wright brothers' flights at Kitty Hawk in 1903, the early decades of the twentieth century were an exciting time for mechanically minded young boys, and Lloyd's fascination with cars knew no bounds. Although Miles clearly benefitted from his son's enthusiasm—Lloyd willingly chauffeured his father back and forth between Encinitas and San Diego before teaching him how to drive himself—he did not encourage it. He was concerned about the foul language used at Warner Rathyen's local Midnite Garage, where Lloyd spent all of his spare hours, and he was also likely displeased that tinkering with cars was distracting his son from mastering the family trade. In no uncertain terms, he ordered Lloyd to stay away from the garage.

Unfortunately for all concerned, his admonition went unheeded. One day, Miles assigned Lloyd the task of watching the flour mill while he attended to other business. Lloyd, anxious to go to the garage, promptly transferred the responsibility to Miles Justus. The mill blew up on his little brother's watch at almost the same moment that their father returned home. Miles, tracking down his errant older son at the garage, gave him a whipping that he never forgot.

Family accounts would differ about what happened next. Lloyd would maintain that he left home of his own accord while Dorothy and Miles Justus would insist that their father told him to pack his bags and never come back. Whatever the true circumstances, Lloyd, then no older than fourteen, left home—and childhood—forever. For some days or weeks, he bunked with various friends and relatives throughout town—including Miles's colorful uncle Jess Thebo—likely hoping that his father would experience a change of heart and ask him back. Such an overture was not forthcoming, however, and Lloyd eventually struck out for San Diego to realize his dream of becoming a professional mechanic.

Despite his diminished workforce, Miles achieved admirable professional success by making the best use of what manpower he had—Murl's full-

Kelloggs and cars. *Author's collection.*

Top: Miles Justus and Dorothy. *Author's collection.*

Bottom: The partially converted Hammond Hotel (*left*) and restaurant built by Kellogg & Son along Highway 101. *Author's collection.*

time labor and Miles Justus's afterschool contributions—and by becoming a consummate recycler. The hard school of experience had taught him that circumstances could change in the blink of an eye, and he would not let present good fortune lull him into a false sense of security. He continued to adhere to lifelong practices of thrift. If any lumber was going spare, he could find a use for it and, more often than not, make something entirely new from it. In fact, he became so famous for his economical ways that, decades after his death, he would be known as Encinitas's "ultimate recycler."

The town witnessed firsthand Miles's penchant for recycling through his renovations of the Hammond Hotel. What was originally an elegant (albeit somewhat dilapidated) three-story building with a mansard roof he gradually transformed into an ordinary-looking stucco structure, whose style blended in with that of his signature "old Spanish" design seen throughout the town. Whenever he ran short of ready lumber, Miles would scavenge it from the hotel's ornamental, or nonessential, architectural details. He first altered the building's appearance by removing its second-story bay windows. As time went on, he made more radical changes. The hotel's ultimate transformation took place in 1924, the same year that he built his strip mall onto its back wall, along Highway 101.[102] That summer, the *Oceanside Blade* reported: "M.M. Kellogg, pioneer lumberman, is busy remodeling

The telephone poles that originally lined Highway 101. *Author's collection.*

Miles's log cabin in Leucadia, built in the 1920s from the discarded Highway 101 telephone poles. *Author's collection.*

his property, the former Encinitas Hotel. Store rooms in the ground floor are being modernized with plate glass fronts and the entire building will be given a coat of stucco."[103] Miles, on discovering an infestation of bats in the third story, tore off this level completely and converted the building into a two-story, flat-roofed structure. Using the salvaged lumber, he built the first silent movie theater in Encinitas on the adjacent street corner, where his carpenter's and blacksmith's shops had once stood. He leased the theater for a few years, until the rival La Paloma Theater opened in 1928 and ran it out of business. Refusing to let the space go unused, he then converted the theater into a café.

Miles similarly recycled materials when he erected an altogether remarkable dwelling in nearby Leucadia during the mid- or late 1920s. When the old telephone poles that lined Highway 101 were pulled down, he purchased these and used them to build a delightfully quaint chalet-style log cabin.* This cabin served as his family's main residence for about a year, until he found the daily commute to Encinitas too inconvenient and moved the household back to town.

Having thus honed his recycling abilities to perfection, Miles was fully prepared to take on, just a short while later, what was to become his most ambitious recycling project—the Encinitas Boathouses.

---

* This was not Miles's first log cabin. Possibly inspired by his early years in his father's own cabin in Leelanau, he had also built one in Boulder.

11
THE ROAD TO YESTERDAY

Positioned above Moonlight Beach, where Miles had once gathered rock and kelp, the Boathouses represented the fulfillment of a long-cherished dream. Miles had loved the water from his early days growing up along the shores of Lake Michigan and had always wanted to build a boat of his own. He had also never quite recovered from his disappointment at having to forego the missionary expedition to Central America so many years earlier.

On Second Street in 1925. *Left to right*: Miles, Ruth (holding Edith's daughter Betty), Forest (Edith's husband), Dorothy, Edith, the Whitehouses (Thebo relatives) and Miles Justus. *Author's collection.*

It was a nostalgic trip that fully reawakened his boatbuilding dreams. In 1925, his renovations on the Hammond Hotel finished, the strip mall completed and the bungalow court that he was building on Second Street* well underway, Miles used the final payment he had received from the sale of the Wyoming homestead to finance a trip back east to revisit scenes of his younger days. Departing in mid-June, he traveled via Colorado, where he stayed with his brother Porter in Boulder, and Wyoming, where he visited the old homestead, before arriving in Michigan in early July. Ruth, virtually blind as she was by this time, was unable to accompany him, but Miles enabled her to experience the trip vicariously by sending home frequent missives like this one:

Boulder, Colo.
6-23-25

Dear Wife,

Arrived in Boulder this morning. We passed through 2 cloudbursts—one in Arizona and one in New Mexico. Stayed all night out in the middle of nowhere, between 2 washed out bridges. I took the train in Albuquerque. However, we had a pleasant ride and saw some wonderful country.

Have been looking the town over. Some things look natural. Others have changed. The places on Goss Street and Grove have been kept up and look good. The town has grown mostly up towards the Sanitarium and on University Hill.

Mary looks about the same, only some older. Haven't seen Porter yet, as I arrived about 12:30 and he is at work on University Hill.

It has been pretty dry here until lately. It rained today some. I spent Sunday at Gallup, N.M. with Mr. Corey's brother.† Arrived there Sat. eve. about 10 and left Sunday eve. at 5 p.m.

Don't think I will stay more than two days here. Will drop you a card when I leave for Chicago. Mary says hello.

Much Love,
Miles[104]

---

* This would consist of a large home for his family and four smaller buildings that would house a laundry and Miles's electrical and plumbing supply stores.

† Cory, a dry goods merchant in Encinitas. In 1925, the same year that he took his trip, Miles sold the Hammond Hotel to Cory. Further details about this transaction are found in the chapter "Trials of the Earth."

Miles at the Petrified Forest in Arizona, circa June 1925. *Author's collection.*

Relishing his first proper vacation in years (if not his life), Miles ended up prolonging his stay in Colorado. He took a trip into the mountains with a nephew, attended church on the Sabbath in Boulder, visited the Sanitarium and inspected some of his old houses in Denver.

It was in Michigan, however, that he enjoyed himself the most. After an absence of three decades, he caused an immediate sensation upon his arrival in Benton Harbor. He could not help but be modestly flattered:

> *Sodus, Berrien Co., Mich.*
>
> *Dear Wife & Children,*
>
> *Will now write you a few lines. Would have written before, but I have been so busy meeting relatives I never knew that I have not had time to write.*
>
> *I wanted to surprise them, but I stopped in to a barbershop to get a shave when I got off the boat, and the barber happened to know Jerue's* folks, and, before I could get cleaned up, my clothes pressed, and myself made presentable, the barber had seen someone else and told them I was in town, and it was telephoned over the county that Miles was there from California.*
>
> *Since then, they have kept me busy. I am at Aunt Josephine's and Laura's place, about 4 miles south of King's Landing where we lived. The little house has been enlarged and not enough of it left to recognize. The*

---

* This was Miles's "Uncle Duff" Jerue, the husband of Christiana Thebo's younger sister Maggie.

interurban cars* run by the place, and it is a resort. I would have liked to get a picture of the place but could not.

The house in Benton Harbor where Chester was born is gone with all of the other buildings built at that time, and in their place is a high school building and large brick church. The city is a very beautiful place now.

I visited the House of David—probably will come home with my hair rolled up under my cap and my whiskers a yard long.†

Laurie's husband—that is, who was Laurie Sharai—is running a novelty shop. Laura is helping him in the shop. She has two children—a boy about 8 and a girl about 12. They live with Aunt Jose.

Uncle Manuel and I are going about from place to place, as I could not find many of them alone. Have been out on the bank of the river this morning. After a rain it is sure a beautiful sight. Everything is so green, and the fruit looks fine.

It has not been very warm, just comfortable. Aunt Dellia is living at present with her daughter. They sold their place in town and are having a new house built. Aunt Maggy and Uncle Duff have a new brick hotel. The old frame building burned down soon after we went from Benton Harbor. Their son Louis runs an art store. He is much taken up with my shell wall light—has it lit and hung in his store window.

I may go and see Aunt Olive in Mishawaka, Ind. about 40 miles south but may not as time seems to fly and I feel as though I was loafing too much.

I visited Father's grave Thursday. The cemetery is now full, and they have two more cemeteries east and south of town. The only thing in Benton Harbor that looks natural is the first house I ever built on Brinton Avenue.‡ I got a Kodak picture of it.

I want to visit the little church I built in Benton Harbor tomorrow. It still stands. The front of it is just the same as when I finished it.

I expect to start north in a few days to visit Mother's grave and the place I spent most of my boyhood days. What few years I could call my boyhood days, as I had none practically after my 12th year.

Will close. Haven't heard from you since leaving. Tell Murl to write Gen. Delivery, Benton Harbor.

Much love to all.

Affectionately,
Miles[105]

---

* A kind of electric streetcar popular in early-twentieth-century America.

† Organized in Benton Harbor, this commune prohibited male members from shaving.

‡ Likely Britain Avenue.

Outside the Jerue House in Benton Harbor: Miles (*standing, center*) with Mrs. Whitehouse (*far left*) and his "Uncle Duff" Jerue (*seated*), owner of the hotel. *Author's collection.*

Waves of nostalgia swept over Miles as he journeyed north to visit his father's relatives in Leelanau, but his most poignant experience was exploring his old childhood haunts in Ludington. This inspired him to write a sentimental poem titled "Memories":*

> *I am wandering today through the old home town*
>   *As I dream of the years gone by.*
> *I gaze o'er the streams and the clear, placid pools*
>   *Where we oft went to swim, my brother and I.*
> *In my memory I see the old apple tree*
>   *And the bank of the lake nearby.*
> *Now many years dead, to its shade none e'er tread,*
>   *As the Indians who planted it and lie buried near it,*
> *Their memory forgotten and fled.*
>   *There's Père Marquette Lake, where we oft went to skate*
> *And in summer we sailed and were gay.*
>   *The lake's still the same, but few boats remain;*
> *The docks gone to rot and decay.*
>   *The old saw mill and the deep sawdust fill,*
> *Where once we romped and played,*

---

* Written in July 1925 in Ludington, Michigan.

Miles *(far right)* with relatives in Northport, Michigan. *Author's collection.*

Now with weeds overgrown, its place no more showing,
The mill gone to rust and decayed.
　Just above the old mill stood our house on the hill
With its garden and flowers and lawn.
　Now with grass overgrowing, no blossoms now showing,
Even the house itself is now gone.
　The little schoolhouse on the hill
Is standing there still.
　Alone it has weathered the years,
And in memory my eyes fill with tears,
　For there's none that remain
Who with us played the games,
　For it's upward of forty long years.
There's the little churchyard
　Just across from the school.
Oh, what sorrow it brings to my mind.
　There mother dear rests, waiting the call of the blessed,
And her memory round my heart is entwined.

Returning home again by way of Colorado and Wyoming, Miles arrived back in Encinitas in mid-August. He shared his cross-country experiences with the *Coast-Dispatch*, which reported:

M.M. Kellogg, well known Encinitas business man, has returned from what he terms "just a wonderful visit" to the east. Kellogg was gone for nearly two months and spent some time in his old home in Michigan. In spite of all of the charms of the eastern states, Kellogg says that he is more than glad to be back in "Sunny California." Scores of his old friends whom he saw on his visit expressed the desire to make California their home.[106]

Once home, Miles could not stop thinking about his trip. It had been a veritable journey back in time, and it had given him a new lease on life. As he had journeyed steadily eastward, it had seemed to him as if he was growing younger and younger until, on reaching Michigan, he was once again in his early twenties, unencumbered by family responsibilities and with his future a blank slate on which anything might be written. As he had attended Sabbath services in the little Adventist church in Benton Harbor, likely singing some of the same hymns that had won him to Adventism, his thoughts had been drawn back to happier days when building boats and sailing the world had seemed very real possibilities.

He still had boats on his mind when he purchased the defunct Moonlight Beach Dance Pavilion and its attached bathhouse around the fall of 1928.[107] (Miles and Murl had built this bathhouse, which consisted of just two dressing rooms—one for men and one for women—and a couple of showers, circa 1920.) With help from Murl and Miles Justus, Miles dismantled the buildings and toted the lumber into town, only to discover that the oddly shaped pieces of wood from the pavilion could not be used for a traditional house as he had intended.* Miles, true to form, was unwilling to let perfectly good materials go to waste, and by the next year, he had hit on a novel idea. In October 1929,[108] he designed and built two boat-shaped houses on Encinitas's Third Street. He did not use any plans but instead relied solely on his ingenuity and long years of experience.†

For the construction, Miles enlisted the reluctant assistance of his youngest son. The teenaged Miles Justus had recently graduated from Oceanside-Carlsbad High School and was just as obsessed with motors as his brother

---

* The pavilion had "studding" and a low ceiling all around its outside.

† The dates of the Boathouses' construction have been a matter of much speculation and controversy, largely due to a proliferation of misinformation circulated by newspapers. For many years, the most reliable information was that supplied by Miles Justus Kellogg. As an elderly man, Miles Justus provided the only existing firsthand account of their construction, recording that they were built from 1927 to 1928. The author has subsequently discovered both an article in the *Coast-Dispatch* archives and a letter written by Miles Minor Kellogg that reliably date the Boathouses' construction to the fall of 1929, with perhaps a few finishing touches being added in 1930.

The Boathouses, shortly after their construction. The original masts and anchors are in place. *Author's collection.*

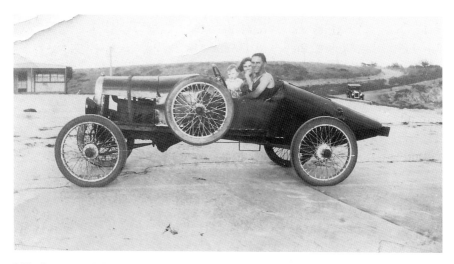

Miles Justus, aged sixteen, and Dorothy seated in his first sports car, which he built from a 1912 Model T Ford. *Author's collection.*

Lloyd had been. Only fourteen when he had begun driving, Miles Justus loved tinkering with cars and had a knack for transforming conservative Model T Fords into flashier and more youthful sports cars. In 1927, two years before work on the Boathouses began, he had played hooky to see his hero Charles Lindbergh and his *Spirit of St. Louis* in San Diego before pilot and plane embarked on their legendary transatlantic flight.* Working on his father's Boathouses was, by contrast, a decidedly unglamorous experience.

There were other reasons, too, for Miles Justus's lack of enthusiasm. He claimed that he was consistently assigned what he called "all the dirty work," while his father reserved the more creative, skilled tasks for himself. Miles Justus later said, "I remember him laying [out] what we call the ribs and the keel—everything out right down in the front down over where the Boats are now on 3rd Street....I had learned before that to do the plumbing and the wiring and the stucco....I stuccoed the bottoms—we called them stucco (they're plastered)—painted, I helped put up the anchors, I helped put up the masts, and I worked on the inside."[109] Any words of protest were ignored. Whenever Miles Justus complained that he didn't want to learn to do a certain task, his father would retort, "Learn it anyhow. It might come in handy someday."[110]

---

* Skipping school along with Miles Justus was his best friend, Pete Lux. Miles Justus's brother-in-law Forest McWhinny was connected to Charles Lindbergh through his mother, who had been a foster daughter of Lindbergh's great-grandparents in Michigan.

Furthermore, Miles never paid his sons for their labor unless they had families to support. Since Miles Justus would not marry until after his father's retirement in the early 1930s, all of his work went unpaid. He later grumbled that all he ever got from his father was *possibly* a suit of clothes to graduate in.

But with the Boathouses, Miles Justus was treated to a pleasant surprise. While helping his father and brother dismantle the pavilion, he made a lucrative discovery: Located at the pavilion's entrance, where admission fees had been collected, were some two-by-six pieces of lumber with large cracks between them. When he ran the sand under these boards through a wire mesh, he found money—lots of twenty-five-cent pieces.

Miles Justus upon his graduation from Oceanside High School in 1928. *Author's collection.*

At the same time, Miles Justus could not help but be impressed by his middle-aged father's skill in designing and constructing the Boathouses. He recalled, "Now, I don't know anything about boats, and I was just wondering how, when he put those anchors on those, how in the world [the shores] were going to hold up like that."[111] To his awe, the Boathouses were still standing, almost exactly as his father had designed them, when he visited Encinitas sixty years later.

Once the Boathouses were finished, Miles believed that their unique designs would attract tenants.[112] Lined on both sides with portholes and boasting redwood anchors, masts and bowsprits,* they were fully outfitted with the amenities of more traditional homes in their approximately 1,100 square feet of living space. The "hull," or first floor, of each Boathouse included a living room, dining room, bedroom and kitchen.† The "deckhouse," or second floor, accessible by a narrow staircase, featured another living room (complete with built-in bookcases), another bedroom and a canopied "deck," or wraparound porch.

Despite such attractions, however, the Boathouses were commercial failures. And for this, Miles held the editor of the *Coast-Dispatch* to blame.

---

* These features were subsequently removed, the anchors allegedly as a result of termite infestations.

† The kitchen includes a captivating detail: A "ship's ladder" leads up to a skylight "hatch" and has "rungs" that can serve as large spice rack shelves.

"NOAH" AND HIS "ARKS"

T he Boathouses instantly attracted curiosity from throughout the South Coast. Ordinarily, Miles might have been pleased, if not flattered, by the unsolicited press coverage that resulted, but the editor of the local newspaper went too far when he exploited Miles's religious beliefs for the sake of a small, amusing write-up.

The Encinitas Boathouses were not the first boat-shaped buildings to appear in San Diego County. About thirty years earlier, a unique abode had been built for Anna Held, founder of an artists' colony, on her cliffside property in La Jolla. The front of the house resembled that of a traditional dwelling but jutting out at the back was a boat-shaped room that overlooked the Pacific Ocean. Thus what made Miles's Boathouses exceptional was not their design alone but also their architect's reputation as an unapologetic Christian and dedicated Bible scholar.

The Kellogg family's ritual of Sabbath keeping was a well-known fact in Encinitas. Whenever anyone hired Miles to do construction work, he or she could expect him to work hard until the project was finished from Sunday to Friday—but not on Saturday. Every week, from Friday sundown to Saturday sundown, every member of the Kellogg household ceased all kinds of labor and secular activity. Not only that, but Miles also apparently openly expressed his belief that Saturday—and not Sunday—was the correct Sabbath for Christians to keep, a practice that may have alienated more mainstream believers. He wrote at one point:

I have listened to arguments pro & con on the Sabbath question and, not being a member of any church, denomination, or creed, I believe I can think and speak in an unbiased way on the subject.

I would ask: Has the time come that we do not need the memorial of the true God and only God of Creation and want to swap it off for a substitute and [have] named often a substitute God?

There [have] been many memorials set up by man but none so eternally lasting as the memorial of creation. Memorials of wood, stone, or metal in time will rust, erode, or decay by the action of the elements. But a piece of time will last with eternity and can be observed and [properly] kept on any part of the globe and its measurement recognized as long as this world revolves on its axis and the sun rises in the East and sets in the West.

Now, if a friend would give you many good gifts and the last one he gave you he would put his name upon it, that you might remember the giver, would you want to swap it for another which had on it the name of someone else who had never given you anything? Would you not consider one who [had] done this an ingrate and lacking respect and loyalty to his friend?

Yet this appears to me to be what the majority of the human race [is] attempting to do. They say that memorial was only given to a certain class of people. The Jew-Christ, the acknowledged agent of the Giver and Creator, says it was given for man, and Christ, being the special agent of

Miles built boats like this for rowing on Lake Hodges. *Left to right*: Vera, Vera's boyfriend Lowell Butler, Edith's brother-in-law Roy Clint, Edith's daughter Betty. *Author's collection.*

the Giver, he ought to know. I would ask: Is the Jew only a man and the Gentile some other kind of animal? I choose to believe I am a man as much as the Jew. Some say they keep the substitute memorial because Christ rose from the dead on that day. I would ask: Why discard the memorial of Creation to give Christ a memorial of His resurrection when He Himself instructed a memorial of that particular event?

There is a multitude of Scripture to prove that the memorial of Creation is still in existence and will be in the regenerated world but nothing to prove the authenticity of the substitute but tradition and the very name of the substitute Sun's Day, originally dedicated to the sun god of the heathen nations.

This question appears to me to be a very weighty one and well answered by the apostles and Christ himself, and there appears to be a few people in the world that refuse to be led by tradition when it is in direct opposition to the demands of the Creator.[113]

Miles broadcasted his faith in other ways as well. In 1925, the same year he traveled back to Michigan, he placed a scripturally based advertisement in the *Coast-Dispatch*:

Real Estate

Some *of our local agents haven't gotten listed, which is very cheap; best of Title, handled only by the Celestial Real Estate Co.*

Insuring *every Subscriber a Home clear from weeds, taxes and mortgages. Farms patterned after the Garden of Eden. See Isa. 65:17, Rev. 20:1, John 14:1–3.*

Insurance *yes; Eternal home Life Insurance Co. unlimited Eternal Life and Youth assured, and free access to the tree of Life. John 3:16, Rev. 22:2.*

Other *Investments as follows: Oil wells Everlasting Joy Oil Wells. Inexhaustible one hundred percent Oil of Gladness. Ps. 45:7.*

Transportation *system, the meteoric air line reaching all parts of the universe, thousand year stop over privilege. Rev. 14:4.*

Gold *mines, there is something better, there is a City paved with gold with gates of Pearl, and foundations of precious stones. Rev. 22:10–14.*

Cheap *why pass it by, buy while you can.*

Guaranteed *by Jehovah. Mat. 6:19-21.*

M.M. Kellogg[114]

In addition, Miles authored religious skits, including one titled *The Progress of the Pilgrim Time*. The plot follows the protagonist, Pilgrim, as he interviews Old Testament people such as Adam and his sons Cain and Abel to seek "the destiny of Man." In one act, Pilgrim also converses with the famous ark builder, Noah, on the subject of the flood:

> *Pilgrim: Now, Noah, as you have lived in the ages before and after the flood, tell me, if you will, about the great change in the world.*
>
> *Noah: Before the deluge, there were no rainstorms as a mist came up from the earth and watered the ground. And although the sun shone seven times brighter and the moon shone as bright as the sun does now, there was a mist in the atmosphere that energized [sic] the heat, and it never got extremely hot or cold. There was no winter and summer as we have it now, and, as the moon shining equal to our present sun and as it in its orbit swings further north and south, there was no extreme cold, either at the South Pole or North Pole.*
>
> *Pilgrim: Yes, I believe you are right, as explorers in the 20ᵗʰ century have found mammoths in the ice of the north perfectly preserved. Also, there is quite an industry in ivory found in the extreme north from those animals, which species now only inhabit the warm climate of Earth. This is sufficient proof that the extreme north was at one time equal in climate to the southern zone.*
>
> *Also, there are found in the great mountain ranges seashells and fish turned into lime rock in perfect shape, showing that the change was instantaneous when the mountain was formed of the earth's surface, which was one sea fathom. If this change had been a slow evolution, all life would have wasted away and returned to the elements.*
>
> *Noah: When God created the earth, He divided the waters in the firmament and left a protection from extreme heat and cold.*
>
> *Pilgrim: We find also in the earth where great forests of the earth have been covered up in practically all parts of the earth and turned into coal. Also, in the formation of both coal and rock we find the imprint of large ferns which do not exist now.*[115]

Although Miles's outspoken beliefs undoubtedly aroused criticism, it was the reputation of his uncle Jess Thebo that drew bona fide suspicions of religious eccentricity in his direction. The scripture-spouting Jess belonged to a group of Spiritualists based in Leucadia, and he was said to have made a table walk on its legs in nearby Spook's Canyon. A self-proclaimed prophet,

Miles's colorful uncle Jess Thebo and his wife, Maggie. *Author's collection.*

Jess would eventually befriend another man who claimed to be the "Son of God" and who would effectively—and tragically—convince Jess to become his unpaid servant and financial backer.

The outcome of this family reputation for religious zeal was, perhaps, inevitable. George S. Breidford, the editor of Encinitas's *Coast-Dispatch*, could not resist taking advantage of such excellent grist for his mill after the Boathouses began taking shape.

Breidford and Miles had clearly enjoyed an amicable relationship at the time of the *Coast-Dispatch*'s inception in 1925. Miles had built the newspaper's office and advertised frequently in the paper. Breidford had reciprocated by faithfully updating the local community on the progress of Miles's building projects and on the comings and goings of various members of the Kellogg family. But by 1927, the two men had had a falling out. Miles was no longer advertising in the paper, and mentions of his family in the *Coast-Dispatch* were relatively few and far between—at least until the fall of 1929.* In the last issue before he signed the paper over to new owners, Breidford made a swipe at his former friend by writing, "M.M. Kellogg and son are building two gigantic boats, resembling in some respects the traditional Noah's Ark, on property owned by the Kellogg's [*sic*], on Third street. The boats are finished inside like ordinary apartments and will be used as such."[116]

Miles was livid. He took the write-up as a deliberate attempt on Breidford's part to damage his business prospects. His ire increased a year and a half later when the *San Diego Union* ran "Haven for the Faithful," a highly embellished version of the original article that was replete with inaccuracies:

> *Six-years ago M.M. Kellogg, believing the world soon was to come to an end by flood, as the Bible records in the story of Noah, erected two boats on his lot in Encinitas and offered them for sale to "the faithful."*
>
> *At the same time he inserted this ad March 27, 1925, in display space in the* Coast Dispatch, *Encinitas' newspaper:*
>
> [Reprinted here was Miles's religious "Real Estate" advertisement quoted above.]
>
> *The ad was run March 27, 1925, but apparently the faithful did not wish to buy an ark, preparatory to a repetition of the flood which made Noah famous. Mr. Kellog [sic] still owns the boats. Neither, it seems, do the*

---

* When Miles Justus Kellogg was asked years later why so few of his father's building projects were mentioned in the *Coast-Dispatch* during the late 1920s, he cited Miles's differences with Breidford.

faithful care to rent them. They are vacant. In summer, they are rented to an occasional tourist for a short period. The novelty attracts.

All of which has destroyed Mr. Kellog's [sic] faith in the belief of "the faithful," and he declares that he is going to rent them as living quarters as regularly as possible.

"I've done my best," he says sadly, "but I can't afford to have them stand idle. No," he added, "I'm not going to advertise. I ran one ad and it didn't do any good."[117]

The famously touchy Miles left no one in any doubt about his feelings regarding such libel. In a bid both to correct the article's scriptural fallacies and to set the record straight regarding his motivations for building the Boathouses, he fired off a hotly worded rebuttal to a rival newspaper:

In answer to the write-up and display of my boat houses at Encinitas appearing in a recent issue of the San Diego Union, especially the write-up, would say that the writer should be highly commended for his literary talent. Do not see how he escaped being President of the United States; at least the president of some city garbage collection agency. He is all wrong about the need of a Noah's Ark, for the next destruction of the earth will be by fire, and then he will need an asbestos suit.

Now, my dear little boy, you should not prevaricate so, for the Scriptures say you shouldn't, and gives such boys a certain name that do so. You will find your true name in (Revelations 21 and 8), so you see you will need that asbestos suit. Now, you can get some fourth-grader to help find that for you. That boomerang you threw at a certain class of people over my head will surely return with interest. They will not feel disposed to patronize your paper or those who carry an ad. in same.

When I came to Encinitas about seventeen years ago I hadn't driven myself out of other towns by such unethical ways of doing business; neither did I solicit money from the public to start my business. Neither had I to buy off opposition to try and get a strangle hold on the public. Put this in your pipe and smoke it with a little opium, and have another pipe dream.

The last end of your literary attempt shows your tender spot, when you say that I withdrew my advertisement, which I discovered, like many others, was all one-sided profit. Now human beings are generally born with a little gray matter underneath their cranium, unless it happens to be an abortion. There appears to be also other exceptions to the rule, and that cavity is filled with jelly and dollar marks; and when I withdrew my ad. the dollar marks

The Boathouses, as seen from Second Street. *Author's collection.*

caused a commotion with the jelly, and it spilled over. All of which caused that wonderful literary production.

We are still living under the law of the survival of the fittest, and when a man in business has lost one-third of the goodwill the rest, in time, will follow suit.

Now, a word of warning to those that use your ad. space. Don't by any means cease to pay tribute to Caesar. Behold, what a great calamity has overtaken me! My posterity will be contaminated to the fourth generation.

The said editor had a chance about eighteen months ago, when those so-called arks were built, to put a cut of them in his paper and give a gentlemanly write-up, as the Los Angeles Examiner *did last Sunday, and it would have been no discredit to his paper and the community. However, that would have cost money for the cut, so he gets another paper to furnish the cut and he furnishes the would-be ridicule.*

Now, I admit the real estate article which bears my name. This was written to combat the high-powered salesmanship being used to legally rob the people. Selling real estate at a much inflated value and getting a payment down, which was forfeited when they discovered that they were misled, which did considerable harm to the locality; and caused them to boost the wrong way for Encinitas. Some of those boomers would have attempted to make people believe that in a short time Los Angeles would be in our suburbs in the North and San Diego would be in our suburbs on the South, and that those that bought property would be in on the ground floor.

Yet, I still believe in the future of Encinitas.

Now, my dear editor, if I can in any further way help you [win] the good-will of the people, do not be bashful in calling on me.

Yours very, very truly,

P.S.

I am sending you a copy of this for your private files, that in the future, if you forget what manner of animal you are, you may refresh your memory.[118]

The "Arks." *Encinitas Historical Society.*

Not surprisingly, the periodical to which Miles submitted this tirade would consent to publish only a milder version of it:

To the people of this district...

In answer to an article accompanying a cut of my boat houses appearing in The San Diego Union *will say that the writer should be commended and exonerated in defending the public against such a villainous attempt to despoil the exquisite surroundings of this beautiful city. However, he seems to have his lines crossed in regard to the building of those boats, for the scriptures state that the next destruction of the earth will be by fire and not by another flood. The writer feels so sorry for that editor that he is contemplating the construction of an asbestos suit for that poor vermiform.*

The building of those boats has helped the building up of Encinitas as much as any editor that has come to town, and the builder was here when there was only one store and business in town and has succeeded very well. However, he didn't succeed by ridicule or by trying to run other people's business, and when he refused to "pay tribute to Caesar" and buy something from the said editor that he did not need, a commotion was started under the craneum [sic] of that certain editor or one of his sattilites [sic],—wherefore that wonderful, intellectual display of literature. The attitude of that certain paper from which sprang or instigated that write-up which accompanied the cuts of those boat houses appears to be trying to repeat former performances and run himself out of town. He has caused about one-third of the business men of the town to love him so much that he is liable to be smothered with their affections and he will have to flee to save himself. He should be commended for warning the public of such a dangerous man that builds dwellings in the form of boat houses to rent.

I did write a real answer to that certain write-up about the boats, but Mr. Wood, Editor of the Progress, thought it so hot that it would burn up the press or set fire to the building, so I had to cool it down. I have concluded to consider the source from which it came as the boy did when he was kicked by the jackass.

Will further say that it is well known that I do not belong to any church, denomination, or creed. Neither do I have a special one of my own to advocate, and said write-up was in part a boomerang thrown at a certain class of people over my head but it will return with interest.

M.M. Kellogg[119]

Unfortunately, the matter did not end there. The story of a modern "Noah" was too good for other periodicals to pass up, and it spread across the nation, with new "facts" about Miles and the Boathouses being "uncovered" every time. Two years after the publication of the *Union* article, an equally misleading write-up appeared in San Diego's *Evening Tribune*: "Although M.M. Kellog [*sic*], former captain, no longer sails the seas, he relives those days in two houses facing the sea, side by side, built to resemble boats. Shrubbery at the foundations make the 'land boats' appear to be cutting the waves."[120]

But the greatest insult of all, as far as Miles was concerned, was a comparison drawn between him and a certain "Captain" William Lound Greenwood of Olympia, Washington. Greenwood, who was portrayed by the press as a religious eccentric, had allegedly predicted that the end of the world would come by worldwide flood around the early 1930s. With this apocalypse in mind, he had begun fashioning an "ark" several years earlier and was spending whatever time he could spare from its construction going around the countryside, "exhorting [people] to repentance."[121] According to reporters, Greenwood even claimed that God had spoken to him personally:

Questioned concerning the visitation, "Captain" [Greenwood] says: "There will be great destruction. The coast land will sink up as far as the Cascade Mountains all the way from North Canada to the south of California. Between the coast and the mountains will be the place of dead bodies.

"San Francisco will not sink until the third shock. The mountains near Bellingham will burst forth and the city will sink. I will warn them in time to flee, but many will not hear. Many will sink with the houses and property, before they will leave them."

[Greenwood] is utterly convinced of the importance of his mission. But he is unable to mention the time of the catastrophe. He alleges to have had conversations with the Almighty on the subject.

"In one of my visions," [Greenwood] says, "the Lord revealed to me the nearness of the sinking of this coast. I asked, 'Lord, how long the hour?' and the Lord replied, 'It was half out in 1927. That was twelve years from the beginning of it.' Then, I told the Lord, it can't be more than twelve years more, and the Lord replied and said, 'Stop there. You know I have told you that I will not tell you the day nor the hour until just before the last, for it would spoil your faith to know the exact time. No man knows the hour of the Lord's coming, but I stand with one foot on the land and one foot on the sea and swear that time shall be no more. Continue to feast upon my holy word.'"[122]

The comparison between Greenwood and Miles was, of course, ludicrous. Miles had never made a similar prediction about an impending destruction by flood, let alone offered this as his reason for building his Boathouses. Moreover, Greenwood's "ark" (which, unlike the Boathouses, was actually intended to sail) was a ramshackle affair. Greenwood clearly knew little about the practicalities of boatbuilding. In sharp contrast to Miles's neatly designed and executed Boathouses, Greenwood's "ark" was a bizarre hodgepodge of mismatched architectural designs.

Rendering the association with Greenwood all the more odious were published photographs of Greenwood, one of which captured him outlandishly rigged out as a kind of frontiersman—bearded and dressed in garb that might have been worn by Buffalo Bill, complete with leather fringe, but with a top hat, instead of a slouch hat, perched atop his head.[123] Miles, who tended to be tidily attired and clean-shaven except for a mustache, could not help but take the comparison extremely personally.

Nevertheless, Miles had learned by this time that losing his temper would not help him achieve his ends. The supposedly anonymous letter that he drafted to one magazine editor had an extremely personal quality that plainly betrayed its author, yet it was much more politely worded than his earlier submissions had been:

May 19, 1931

Mr. Theo Ward
Editor of the Idealist Magazine

Dear Editor (a private letter to you)
I have been wondering if you realize that the write-up appearing recently in your magazine concerning Mr. M.M. Kellogg of this town is all a falsehood.
I understand that a reporter of a certain San Diego newspaper obtained Mr. Kellogg's picture and the cut of his Boats through false pretenses and probably came to you the same way.
Mr. Kellogg has been a contractor and builder in this town for many years, and the people here and in other towns near—yes, even in San Diego and Los Angeles—know that those Boat house apts. were built for rental purposes only. Being built in lots on a hill and overlooking the ocean, they were also built as a novelty and to have something different than just apartment houses.
Mr. Kellogg does not profess to be a prophet nor classes himself with the said Mr. Greenwood of Olympia, Washington, mentioned in your write-up. I understand you know his history so why should I judge the write-up

Miles and Ruth around the time of the Boathouses' construction. *Author's collection.*

in your magazine will not injure Mr. Kellogg, as much as it may those who read and believe it to be true, as the prophecy by the Revenites did a few years ago?

Mr. Kellogg is not a member of any church or denomination. He reads the Bible and believes it. Therefore, he knows the world will never be destroyed by flood again.

He does not think that anyone should set a date for the Lord's return. God alone knows the hour and the day.

I would advise you and a reporter of a certain San Diego newspaper to correct the mistake you have made in writing up this false statement. I think it would be a great benefit to you as an editor of your magazine and also in your business.

Someday and somehow, truth will win. It always does.

A Reader.[124]

But all of Miles's attempts to set the record straight proved futile. The story of "Noah" and his "arks" would remain firmly attached to the Boathouses, not only for the rest of Miles's life but also for nearly a century to come.

Nor could he afford to waste much more time fretting over his reputation. Circumstances beyond his control were steadily propelling him toward retirement and toward abandoning Encinitas, his home of over fifteen years, for a ranch near the Mexican border. His career—and life—were swiftly drawing to a close.

TRIALS OF THE EARTH

The unwelcome press coverage of the Boathouses was not the only thorn in Miles's side. Slander might be irritating and sensation-seeking reporters obnoxious, but they were nothing compared to the real troubles that began to plague him as the prosperous 1920s gave way to a new and altogether dismal decade. Recurrent financial reverses, the onset of the Great Depression, an ever-widening array of health problems and anxieties over his grown children's welfare would gradually converge to bring about both the end of his career and his premature death.

Miles, for all his talents as a builder and inventor, lacked other practical attributes. For one thing, he was not a particularly shrewd businessman. All too frequently, his careless or informal methods of lending and borrowing money—not to mention his misplaced trust in his fellowmen—placed his financial future in jeopardy or, at the very least, left him seriously out of pocket. Due to his own history of straitened circumstances—times of desperation when no one had offered him a helping hand—Miles was the soul of generosity. He would lend money, interest free, to anyone in need. Among those who borrowed regularly from him was Sydney Chaplin, the older half-brother and business manager of silent film star Charles Chaplin. Syd, who lived in a tiny house south of Miles's plumbing supply house, had a talent for letting money slip through his fingers. Whenever he found himself caught short, he would approach Miles for a loan. Syd, to his credit, always repaid the money, but Miles's no-interest policy meant that he never profited from these transactions. Miles also borrowed freely

Miles's "bungalow court" on Second Street. The family lived in the house at right. Syd Chaplin lived just down the street. *Author's collection.*

himself—from both friends and the bank. Ostensibly, he owned numerous properties scattered throughout Southern California, but by the time of the great Stock Market Crash in 1929, every one of these was mortgaged to the hilt.

Miles's naivete, however, could not be blamed for all of his financial misfortunes. One factor over which he had limited control was his neighbors' unethical methods of transacting business. Frequently, a customer would be either unable or unwilling to pay hard cash for his goods or services, thereby compelling him to accept payment in kind. Miles consequently ended up with a motley assortment of stocks for commercial ventures, such as German forest industries, that all too often proved worthless.

Even worse, some customers never paid at all. Various neighbors—most notably, the town postmaster—would hire Miles to do work or would take lumber from his lumberyard, only to refuse to pay afterward. In the late 1910s, the postmaster had even stooped to defrauding Lloyd, then just a young boy, when he hired him to plow his fields. Every day for three months, Lloyd had faithfully worked two horses with a single plow, getting up at six o'clock in the morning and returning home at six o'clock at night. He was still so small that he had to stand on an apple cart so that he could pass the harnesses over the horses' heads. In the end, the postmaster refused to pay Lloyd. Miles had become indignant on his son's behalf and had confronted the man, but his efforts to extract payment for either Lloyd's work or his own proved futile.

The most shocking swindle of all, however, occurred with the sale of the renovated hotel building. In 1925, Miles sold the Hammond Hotel to Cory, a local dry goods merchant who proved to be just as unscrupulous as the postmaster. Not only did Cory refuse to pay Miles for his purchase, but he also allegedly went as far as to secure a judgment absolving him from payment on rather astonishing grounds: A bedstead that Miles had left in one of the hotel rooms prevented him from renting out the room—or so Cory claimed.

Miles's sense of justice was outraged by such trickery. He had never recovered from the swindle in Colorado that had robbed him of his valuable real estate, and the discovery that dishonesty was just as rampant in California had a demoralizing effect. It was around this time that he began making inquiries into the possible recovery of the Fort Morgan ranch that he had lost so many years earlier to the attorneys. He found a prime opportunity for doing so when he learned that the son of a La Jolla client had a law practice in northern Colorado and could look into the matter for him. This new attorney was optimistic. After examining the relevant documents, he advised Miles that the statute of limitations had not yet run out and that it might still be possible to recover his property. This news should have encouraged Miles, but the reopening of the incident evidently proved to be too troubling for him because, in the end, he declined to pursue the matter further. He told the attorney to "forget it," that he had "had enough," while observing, with a curious blend of bitterness and hopefulness, that there would be "no lawyers in heaven."[125]

Of all the financial disappointments that the 1920s brought, however, it was the stock market crash, ushering in the Great Depression, that dealt Miles the harshest blow. He, like many others, had invested money in the local building and loan company, and he lost his entire investment when it failed. With a mortgage taken out on virtually every property that he owned, he lived in constant fear of foreclosures, and unable to find tenants for his many rental properties, he was soon scrambling to gather the necessary funds to hold on to his real estate.

In seeking a solution to these troubles, he turned to the people on whom he had the greatest claim—his children and their spouses. He had always been generous in offering his grown sons and daughters real estate or other valuable gifts, so his pleas were not ignored.* Those who could afford it helped

---

* Among other things, he had made Chester frequent loans and given him a truck upon his marriage, had gifted land to Irma and had offered Lloyd real estate—an offer that Lloyd had declined.

Miles Justus's home on Second Street. The Boathouses can be seen in the block behind. *Author's collection.*

him as they could. Edith lent him the money to pay off the mortgage on his plumbing supply house and attached buildings, Lloyd gave him money to secure other properties, Dorothy kept his Modern Woodmen of America insurance paid up and Miles Justus, to whom Miles owed money, forgave the debt so that his father could pay his taxes.[*]

Even with this assistance, Miles was forced to part with a number of properties, including the Boathouses. When he failed to find tenants for them, he traded the Boathouses for land in Escondido. As it would transpire, in this transaction Miles was defrauded yet again. The property in Escondido consisted of two pieces of land on the top of a mountain, around the base of which the popular bandleader Lawrence Welk owned property.[†] It had never been surveyed, however, and Miles never received a deed to the land. Consequently, when another man claimed it after Miles's death, his children were unable to prove ownership.

Equally distressing to Miles were the financial plights of dear friends and neighbors. James Rupe was a case in point. The Kelloggs had lived down the street from the Rupe family during their near-decade residence

---

[*] Miles Justus had by this time begun working for August Anderson, a Swedish-born contractor in Encinitas.

[†] This was the Lawrence Welk Resort. Murl and his wife would vacation there during their retirement.

in the Hammond Hotel, and the two families were good friends. The Rupe children had been playmates of the youngest Kellogg children, and James's wife had sewed Dorothy's graduation dress for Ruth. Moreover, Miles respected the Rupes for being an exemplary Christian family. In 1928, James Rupe commissioned Miles to build a chic, brand-new building in the then-fashionable Art Deco style to house his dry goods store.[126]* The construction costs totaled around $10,000.[127] When the stock market crashed the following year and Rupe repeatedly failed to make the payments, Miles was forced to take over the building from his friend and run the dry goods business himself until he found a buyer six months later.[128]

But Miles had more than money troubles weighing on his mind. Just as troubling as the chaotic state of his finances was his deteriorating health—an ever-insistent harbinger of his rapidly approaching end. Now in his late fifties, he was beginning to feel the effects of a lifelong health history characterized by hard physical labor, chronically poor stress management and—above all—a fondness for smoking. On his conversion to Adventism as a young man, Miles had conscientiously adhered to the church's health guidelines. Following his split from the church, however, he had gradually slipped back into his old smoking habits. Murl, who was well acquainted with the smell of his father's corncob pipes from years of working alongside him, would later remark that the smoke from them was "so strong it could get up and walk."[129]†

In 1930, Miles was admitted to the Adventists' Glendale Sanitarium and Hospital for an abdominal complaint. Despite the relative gravity of his condition, he was optimistically dismissive of advice to undergo an invasive operation. He even joked about it in a letter home:

Sunday, June 1

Dear Wife & Children,

Just a few lines. Think I am improving but am pretty weak. Edith & Forest have been down twice, and Lloyd has been over twice. He was here about 3. We would have liked to have got out for a ride, but he had some girls with him that wanted to go to a show.

---

* The façade of this building (known as the "Rupe building") has been preserved and can still be seen in historic downtown Encinitas, just a few streets from the Boathouses.

† Miles's attachment to his corncob pipes resulted in household conflict. One day, when Ruth, who found the smelly pipes distasteful, threw one out a window from the hotel's second story, he protested loudly, declaring that the pipe had been "just getting ripe." The only other known argument between Miles and his wife culminated in him stalking out of the house in a huff. Ruth objected, saying, "What will the neighbors think?" Miles retorted, "That's all you ever think about!" He returned home a couple of days later.

Looking east from the intersection of D and Second Streets, 1920s. Rupe's dry goods store is at right. The La Paloma Theatre is at left. *Author's collection.*

Miles and Ruth (*center*) with Edith and Forest on their wedding day in 1920. The ceremony was conducted in the Hammond Hotel's second floor. *Author's collection.*

I will be ready to come home Thursday morning if Miles [Justus] wants to come after me, or I can go up to Edith's for a few days and let him come up next Sabbath. Or maybe I can get Lloyd to take me home. However, there is no hurry. I will be too weak to work, and perhaps I had better stay at Edith's a few days. I can take practically the same treatments at home, and I do not think it advisable to have an operation. Don't think the stone in my bladder will cause any particular trouble. Some day I might be short of stone for foundation. Then I can make use of it.

Much Love to all
Husband & Father
M.M.K.[130]

The bladder stone was removed a couple of years later, around March 1933,[131] Miles's objections notwithstanding, and he cheerfully made the best of the situation. He thriftily had the stone bronzed and then used it as the end of a watch fob.

Still, Miles was not oblivious to his declining health.* He wrote to Edith's husband, Forest, an occasional employee of Kellogg & Son, in 1931:

6-4-31
Brawley

Dear Son Forest,

Find enclosed check for $40.00.

The loan co. only paid ⅓ when [the] roof was on so I couldn't ring in any more. However, I will have another $800 due by the end of next week and will try and get 100 more to apply on the 200.

Have the house plastered, one coat outside garage, and the lath on & windows in. Will have the plaster on by the middle of next week.

Have been feeling better the last two weeks. Guess the hot weather and the amount of water I drink is helping me. However, I get pretty tired. Don't seem to be as young as I used to be.

Give my love to all.

Will send you some more money just as soon as I can.

Father K.[132]

---

* Miles was clearly philosophical about aging. He liked to tell the following story: A woman asked her husband to get her a hearing aid. When the husband returned with a hook to go over her ear and a tube to dangle, she objected, "That's no hearing aid!" Her husband insisted that it was, saying that when people saw it, they would think it was a hearing aid and shout.

Above: The house Forest McWhinny built in 1925 near his father-in-law's log cabin in Leucadia. Edith is pictured at left with friends. *Author's collection.*

Left: The merry spinsters: Dorothy (*left*) and Vera. *Author's collection.*

Edith with her daughters, Betty (*left*) and Evangeline. *Author's collection.*

Miles's anxieties about providing for his unmarried daughters only added to his burdens. Both Vera, the family's resident housekeeper, and the more professionally minded Dorothy exasperated their father by steadfastly refusing the many marriage proposals that they received. Following Chester's example, all of the children except Lloyd had attended either the Adventists' San Fernando Academy or Pacific Union College in Northern California—in some cases, both. Miles, who had frowned on all of his children's academic ambitions, held traditional views on women's education and had discouraged his daughters, in particular, from attending college, expecting them to eventually marry and be provided for.* Not until Dorothy, the youngest of the girls, enrolled at Southwestern Junior College in Keene, Texas,† did he help finance a daughter's higher education.

Besides Vera and Dorothy, Miles was worried about Edith. A month after he wrote to Forest, his son-in-law died in a tragic accident. Edith and her two little girls, Betty and Evangeline, left their home in San Fernando the following year to move in with her parents in Encinitas. Miles almost immediately began trying to organize his daughter's life. Introducing her to a local widowed lumberman named Charles Osbeck, he made it clear that he thought Edith should marry him.

---

* When Miles approached Dorothy for a loan to pay his Modern Woodman insurance, he promised her that if she lent him the money, he would pay for her trousseau. Miles thought that this was a safe promise to make. He told Dorothy that she was so particular that he doubted he would ever have to make good on it.

† Present-day Southwestern Adventist University. Chester was then president of the college.

Miles's house in Potrero. *Author's collection.*

Miles had good reason to expect success in his matchmaking. Years earlier, in San Diego, he had effectively broken up Edith's romance with Vinton Wright, the son of Thomas Wright, Edith's landlord and Miles's erstwhile business partner. When the two teenagers had announced their engagement, Miles had refused to give his consent. The young people's romance had withered away, and in 1916, the same year that Miles moved his family to Encinitas, Vinton had married another girl.

The passage of time had made Edith less vulnerable to coercion, however, and Miles's hopes of securing Osbeck for a son-in-law were disappointed. Perhaps from feelings of guilt, Edith proved more malleable in business matters. Miles successfully persuaded her to invest her savings in the piece of countryside property that he had selected for his retirement—forty to sixty acres near a little village called Potrero, about forty miles east of San Diego and just across the border from Tecate, Mexico. With Miles Justus's help, he built a house on the property.*

Construction on the two-story frame house went quickly. By early January 1932, the house was completed, and Miles and Ruth, packing up the Encinitas household, moved with Vera, Edith, Betty and Evangeline into the hills. There, after the grief and turmoil of recent years, Miles hoped to find some personal peace in the quiet of the countryside. Little did he know that he had less than a year to live.

---

* Edith also paid for the lumber with which the house was built, purchasing it from Osbeck at a discount.

THE END TIMES

M iles's choice of acreage was interesting, to say the least. Contemporary photographs show an arid property that was unlikely to support the alfalfa he planted and that was hardly habitable for his Angora rabbits and Buff Orpington chickens—gifts from Vera's boyfriend, Lowell Butler. Moreover, it was surrounded by a rugged topography inhabited by dangerous wildlife and Prohibition-defying bootleggers.

In many ways, this new home was uncomfortably reminiscent of the one that he and the family had known in the bleak Wyoming days. It was even more isolated than the homestead had been, and the nearest neighbors lived four miles away. According to Edith's daughter Betty, this distance from civilization precluded the possibility of even basic amenities: "There was no electricity available then, so my uncle [Miles Justus] used water power to generate it—enough electricity to light up tiny light bulbs that give a dim light. There was not enough electricity for a refrigerator, so the cooling power of evaporation kept our food cool. Grandpa framed a box that was covered with wire and gunny sacking if I remember correctly. It hung from the old oak tree near the kitchen, and water slowly dripped on it."[133] Betty, then a little girl of about seven, had to make her way alone, up and down four miles of rattlesnake-infested gullies and ravines, to get to and from school each day.

There may have been a method to Miles's apparent madness in setting down roots in such an isolated wilderness: his resilient faith. Over the years, he had often questioned the ways of his God. This was especially true where his wife's welfare was concerned. Ruth had lost the remaining sight in one

Above: Miles at work on his ranch. *Author's collection.*

Right: The waterwheel that Miles Justus developed for irrigating his father's land. *Author's collection.*

eye a few years earlier when the cork from a peroxide bottle had popped out and struck it. Her other eye eventually developed sympathetic blindness, after which all she was able to see were shadows—light and darkness. To Miles, once too preoccupied to fully empathize with his wife's handicap, God's apparent condoning of this tragedy was an unfathomable mystery.[*] Edith later remembered, "[It] used to bother my father because he thought the Lord shouldn't have let that happen to her because her eyes weren't very good anyhow. And he felt real bad about the Lord not doing things for her."[134] Yet misfortunes such as this had drawn Miles closer to Ruth in recent years. It was with her by his side that he eagerly looked forward to his well-deserved retirement, and it was she who inspired one of his last poems, "Growing Old Together":

> *Along this life's rough pathway,*
> *We have travell'd hand in hand.*
> *The years they seem much shorter,*
> *As we're nearer now the end.*
>
> *We're growing old together,*
> *We are aging day by day,*
> *Our steps they grow more feeble,*
> *And our hair is turning grey.*
>
> *Our boys and girls are leaving*
> *One by one their childhood home;*
> *Each chair will soon be empty,*
> *When we'll be left alone.*
>
> *We'll miss their cheerful voices*
> *As together they did sing.*
> *The hours they now seem lonely,*
> *But sweet memories they bring.*
>
> *And when this journey's ended,*
> *And we have crossed life's span,*
> *May we be called together,*
> *May we go hand in hand.*

---

[*] Chester would later remark that his father had "known deep sorrow" in life and that he "had loved [Ruth] dearly, but was the head of the house and knew it!"

Vera. *Author's collection.*

At the Potrero ranch. *Left to right*: Miles, Elder Bryant, "Mr. Williams," Vera's boyfriend Lowell Butler and Edith's daughter Evangeline. *Author's collection.*

Along with his devotion to Ruth, Miles's faith in God, too, had strengthened, and he had recently rededicated his life to his Maker. As a result, it was not just retirement to which he looked forward in Potrero but also to having the leisure to witness to others about his faith as he had during his younger days—specifically, by holding Bible studies in the local village.

His feelings of animosity toward the Seventh-day Adventist Church had correspondingly mellowed with the passage of time. Although he remained a staunch nonconformist, he had attended Sabbath services for perhaps the first time in twenty years during his trip east in 1925. He had also rejoiced over Chester's ordination as a minister of the Seventh-day Adventist Church and now welcomed Adventist church elders to his ranch.

Similarly, he had continued to believe in the basic tenets of Adventism. Back in Wyoming, he had witnessed to fellow homesteaders by explaining to them the Adventist interpretations of biblical prophecies. These prophecies included those regarding the so-called End Times, or the events leading up to the end of the world as described in the Book of Revelation. Many Adventists believed that these events would culminate in their flight into remote wildernesses to escape persecution. Future generations would consequently speculate that Miles had selected the Potrero property with the End Times prophecies specifically in mind. It was as if Miles, like

A Potrero family gathering. *Left to right*: Lloyd, Miles, Vera, Edith, Clarence Brown, Helen, Arthur Brown (Helen's husband), unidentified grandchild, Irma, Arthur Williams (Irma's husband). *Author's collection.*

his father before him, had foreseen his rapidly approaching end and then confused it with the end of the entire world. Certainly, his decision to write a poem about the resurrection, "We Shall Sleep,"* suggests that his thoughts were focused on the afterlife.†

Miles did not have long to wait. He had recently made attempts at lifestyle reform—substituting buckwheat blossoms for tobacco in his pipe before ceasing smoking altogether—but these measures came too late. He died on his ranch on December 28, 1933, at the age of just sixty-three.

The end came without warning. Miles, Ruth, Edith, Vera and the little girls had driven to Encinitas to spend Christmas with Murl and his family. A few days later, following a lively afternoon playing baseball with his sons and grandchildren, he returned to Potrero with Ruth and Vera. The day's active exertions took their toll. That night, Ruth knew something was

---

* See page 151.

† In a letter that Dorothy Kellogg wrote to her brother Lloyd in the late 1980s, she remembered, "He [our father] and I were out on the deck of the house in Potrero. He actually pulled me down on his lap and we had a long visit. He had quit smoking, talked to me about his past life, and expressed a desire to go up to the little village of Potrero and give Bible studies….Then shortly after that visit he sent me a long poem he had written and asked me to type it for him. The title of the poem was 'We Shall Sleep But Not Forever' and after each stanza he had a Bible text that referred to what he was endeavoring to express….I was so happy when I received that poem for I knew that he had renewed the relationship he had had with Jesus as a young man, as lay-minister for the Church of God."

The Potrero ranch. *Author's collection.*

terribly wrong when she heard a sudden, strange change in her husband's breathing. Miles had suffered a heart attack.

It fell to Vera to summon help. Going out into the dead of night, she hiked four miles along the highway and through cattle fields until she reached the home of a neighbor, who then called a doctor and rang up Miles Justus in Encinitas. These efforts, however, were in vain. The doctor and Miles Justus arrived in Potrero at the same time, but they were too late. Miles had already died.

We Shall Sleep
By Miles Minor Kellogg

We shall sleep, but not forever,	1 Cor. 15:51,52
In that lonely silent grave—	
Blessed be the Lord of Mercy,	Romans 5:7,8
Blessed be the Christ which saves.	
He has trod the path before us,	Matt. 28:2–6
He has opened wide the tomb,	
He will pardon our transgressions:	
And redemption will be soon.	Isaiah 55:7
We shall sleep, but not forever,	Psalms 4:8
If His will we here obey:	John 2:6
From this earth and its corruption,	Romans 8:21
He will take us home some day.	
Then we'll meet our long lost loved ones,	1 Thess. 4:17
Then we'll know and shall be known:	Prov. 14:32
Then redeemed from death and sickness,	1 Cor. 15:54–56
And the king has claimed His own.	
We shall sleep, but not forever,	Job 33:34
The great ransom has been paid;	Hosea 13:14
On the cruel cross Christ suffered,	1 Tim. 2:6
And a way for us He made.	
He will take us to those mansions—	John 14:1–3
Oh, the half was never told!	
With the prophets and apostles,	Rev. 21:19
We may walk the streets of gold.	
We shall sleep, but not forever—	1 Cor. 15:51, 52
Soon the trumpet it will sound;	1 Thess. 4:14–19
And the dead which sleep in Jesus,	
From all parts of earth are found:	Rev. 21:21
And with them we all shall enter	John 15:13
Pearly gates that open wide;	Eph. 3:17–19
If we here are true and faithful,	
And in His great love abide.	

We shall sleep, but not forever—
 Christ went forth first to prepare;   Eph. 1:7
And with all the holy angels,
 He'll be waiting for us there
On the bank of life's pure river,
 With its fruit of life so fair: Rev. 22:1–5
Yes, the Lamb of Life will light it;
 And there is no night there.

We shall sleep, but not forever—
 From the mountains and the sea,   Rev. 29:13
From the deserts and the valleys,
 From this sin-cursed earth set free;   Rev. 29:12
For the judgment's nearly ended   Dan. 13:1,3
In God's book of life so fair: Rom. 14:10
With the prophets and apostles,   Dan. 7:9,10
 Will our names be written there!   Luke 10:20

We shall sleep, but not forever: Rev. 20:1,2
 Though but mortals now we be,
If our names are still on record,   Rev. 3:5
 Christ's immortals shall be we: 1 Cor. 15:51–54
At the sounding of the trumpet,
 That great change to all will come,—
At that time and that time only,
 We'll be ready for that home.

We shall sleep, but not forever,   John 14:1–3
 Christ, Himself, did so declare;   Rev. 20:6
In His Father's many mansions   Mal. 4:1
 He has gone forth to prepare: Rev. 21:1–3
A thousand years to live in heaven,
 And this earth by fire is cleansed;
It will be like long lost Eden,
 Then to it we shall descend.

We shall sleep, but not forever,
 Job, the prophet, did declare—
Face to face we'll see our Savior,   1 Cor. 13:32

And be welcomed by Him there.   Exodus 33:11
Though the worm destroy this temple,   Matt. 25:34
   And we again return to dust;
We shall be giv'n renewed bodies—   Gen. 3:19
   He is faithful, true and just.

We shall sleep, but not forever,
   In that glorious world made new;
We shall ever love and praise Him
   All the countless ages through:
Where the lamb, the wolf and lion   Isaiah 11:6-9
   Dwell in peace there side by side;
And a little child shall lead them—
   It is there I would abide!

EPILOGUE

In what was to be a final family reunion, Miles's nine surviving sons and daughters gathered for his burial at San Diego's Greenwood Cemetery. As a special tribute, they sang his poem "We Shall Sleep" to the tune Vera had composed, just as they had sung together for so many years around the family organ at home.[135] Chester, along with Edith's brother-in-law Harry McWhinny, conducted the service.[136]

The family was allowed little time to grieve, however. Miles had left his affairs in shambles. Not only had he written no will, but most of his real estate was still mortgaged as well. Miles Justus, to whom the job of settling the estate fell, had to call in various loans and sell most of the properties.

As for Ruth, her life was far from over, and she was forced to adapt to fresh and frequent changes. Edith, realizing that three defenseless women and two small children could not continue to live by themselves in such an isolated location, leased the Potrero property to the United States Border Patrol. She moved everyone back to Encinitas, where she and Vera took over the laundry business that was located in their father's old plumbing supply building on Second Street. The two young women successfully supported themselves, their mother and the two little girls by running the laundry for the next five years of the Depression, until Edith relocated to San Diego around 1938 for her children's education. Ruth, initially remaining behind in Encinitas with Vera, moved to San Diego when Vera married and relocated there two years later. Around 1944, Ruth changed homes a final time when she accompanied Edith and Edith's new husband, Morris Tyrrell, to their pear orchard outside a little town called Placerville, northeast of Sacramento, in Northern California. Vera and Irma eventually joined them there.

The years in Placerville were often desperately unhappy for Ruth. Her blindness beleaguered her by forcing her to depend on Edith for even her most basic needs. She could not wash, dress or feed herself without assistance. Moreover, she was lonely. Edith, although devoted to her mother, had other work to attend to about the house or in the pear orchard. This meant that Ruth was left alone for long stretches of time. Edith later wrote of her mother during this time with regret:

> *She had turned her days into nights and slept most of the day. I told her it was difficult to continue that way for both of us.*
>
> *She said, "How can I keep awake, when no one comes in to talk to me?" And like it is so often, everyone was too busy! She couldn't read, listen to TV, or walk around alone, and the radio wasn't often welcome.*
>
> *After all, what can one expect at 91 years old—and blind!*[137]

It was Ruth's active mind that saved her from utter despair. Poetry, which had always been a source of comfort and strength for her, now became increasingly meaningful to her. She wrote poetry not only to express her emotions and her faith but also to communicate with her children on a personal and individual level. Feeling her way across the paper with her pen, she would painstakingly scrawl out verses and send these to her far-flung children as special tokens of her love. She similarly made a point of nurturing relationships with her many grandchildren and great-grandchildren, some of whom lived too far away to ever visit. Her excellent memory meant that she never forgot an anniversary, and she faithfully sent one dollar—known to the recipients as a "Grandma Dollar"—to each of her twenty-three grandchildren and forty-five great-grandchildren on their birthdays.

At the same time, Ruth took a lively interest in politics and current affairs. Unlike her late husband, she had no qualms about aligning herself with a political party. She was a staunch Republican. Once, while staying with Vera and Vera's husband, Merritt Hocking, during the months leading up to the presidential election of 1960, Ruth, by then almost ninety years old, made her own small but unique contribution to the campaign of Richard M. Nixon, then the U.S. vice president and a native Californian. Delighted that her daughter and son-in-law had taught their parakeet to welcome her

Ruth with her oldest grandchildren in Encinitas. *Author's collection.*

with "Good morning, Grandma!" she expressed a wish that they would also teach him to say, "Vote for Nixon!" Vera and Merritt, although Democrats, obligingly began to do so, only for the bird to come up with his own rendition. One evening, he startled everyone by calling out in a clear voice, "Vote for Nixon, Grandma!"[138]

Above all, Ruth's spiritual life sustained her. Although unable to attend church, she remained a devout Seventh-day Adventist and derived great comfort from having the Adventists' *Review & Herald* read to her.*

Her faith remained strong to the last. Around 1945, she was diagnosed with breast cancer. Edith and Vera, who deprecated conventional treatments, kept the diagnosis from their mother and successfully nursed her for the next seventeen years by administering alternative treatments. They gave her vegetable juices to drink and applied what were known as the Lincoln Bacteriophage Lysates. Consequently, it was of old age and not of cancer that Ruth eventually passed away.

The family had fair warning this time. Just as Miles's father, Justus Abram, had had a premonition of his own demise, in the early months

---

* Over the years, she had especially enjoyed the articles written by the editor, Francis Wilcox, who had conducted her baby son Walter's funeral service years earlier in Boulder.

of 1962, Dorothy had a premonition of her mother's impending death. In a dream, she saw Ruth as a young woman, running down a hill in a graveyard with her hair flying up behind her. Six months later, Ruth died of congestive heart failure on August 30. She had turned ninety-one a few months earlier, but her last words were so strong and clear that they could be heard down the hall: "So hard to die," she gasped. "My dear Jesus... My hope is built on nothing less than Jesus' blood and righteousness...Oh, Jesus, come and get me soon!"[139]

The commemorations of Ruth's life were quiet affairs. A day or two after her passing, a memorial service was held at Memory Chapel in Placerville.[140] Chester, now living on the other side of the country, was unable to perform the ceremony. Dorothy's husband, Wilbur Dunn, and Edith's brother-in-law Harry McWhinny were two of the three Adventist elders who officiated in his stead.[141] A graveside service was later held at the Greenwood Cemetery in San Diego, and Ruth's body was laid to rest beside Miles's.

Despite the passage of almost three decades since his death, Miles's influence continued to be felt throughout the family. When Ruth had written her memoirs in the 1930s, she had reflected on her husband's legacy: "It has been lonely for us without your father...but we know that he is at rest from all worry and sorrow, and we have that blessed hope that if we are faithful here we may meet him again. And there in the new earth he can still continue to build, a house of his liking, all free from debt, a gift of our heavenly Father. May each one of us so live here on earth that we may have a home over there."[142]

With such a heritage to inspire them, all of Miles and Ruth's children led lives consistent with their early instruction in honesty, morality and industry.

Chester (1892–1984), after years of postponing his education for the sake of helping support his parents and younger siblings, ultimately achieved his goal of a college diploma. He graduated with a bachelor's degree from the Adventists' Pacific Union College in 1923. Five years later, at the age of only thirty-six, he became president of present-day Southwestern Adventist University in Keene, Texas. In contrast to his father, he actively encouraged his younger siblings in aspiring to higher education. Wherever they lived, he and his wife, Clara (née Brown), opened their home—no matter how modest or small—to his many brothers and sisters so that they could afford to study at an Adventist school.

With her good looks and hot temper, Irma (1895–1989) was proof that the apple did not fall far from the tree. Considered "worldly" by her more conservative siblings, she inherited Miles's religious perspectives,

Chester working at the craft his father taught him. *Author's collection.*

particularly with regard to the Seventh-day Adventist Church. Following the death of her first husband, Joseph Arthur Williams, in 1946, she moved north from San Diego to live near her mother and sisters in Placerville. There she eventually ceased attending Sabbath services. Nevertheless, her faith remained important to her. When her second husband, Linton Kreinkamp, proposed, she agreed to their marriage only after he promised to become an Adventist.

Edith (1896–1995), the child most similar in personality to Ruth, continued the pattern of service to her family that she had begun on the Wyoming homestead. She daily epitomized one of her favorite mottoes: "What we put out into the lives of others comes back into our own."*

Vera (1900–1997), who had bonded with her father over music, became an amateur composer of religious music.† She set many of her parents' poems to tunes of her own composition and wrote her own songs. Some of these were performed over the radio by the Adventist contralto Del Delker.

---

* Edith's paraphrase of a verse from Edwin Markham's poem "A Creed."

† Wherever he lived, Miles had always insisted on having a piano, and whenever he could be home when Vera was growing up, he had taken the time to teach her the rudiments of piano playing.

Miles Justus (*foreground*) and Murl (*wearing cap*) at work on the Sunnydale dormitories. *Author's collection.*

Besides Miles Justus, Murl (1902–1994) was the only one of Miles's sons to follow in his footsteps as a professional builder and contractor. Moving with his wife, Mabel (née Wood), over fifty times during their married life, Murl worked up and down the State of California, as well as throughout the American Midwest and as far east as Georgia. His many projects included helping build the dormitories of the Adventists' fledgling Sunnydale Academy in Centralia, Missouri.

Helen (1903–1963), helpful like Edith yet painfully shy, took over from Edith as their mother's "right arm" when her older sister left Encinitas to pursue higher education. She went on to marry Chester's brother-in-law Arthur Brown and became a farmer's wife. Unlike her brothers and sisters, Helen did not inherit the Kellogg tendency for longevity, but she did inherit the family's sensitivity for premonitions. At her mother's funeral in 1962, she confided to Dorothy her belief that she would "be next." She died almost exactly one year to the day after her mother's passing.

Lloyd (1905–1997) was the proverbial black sheep of the Kellogg family. Following his premature dismissal from home, he turned his back not only on his father's profession but also on his religious faith. He refused to have anything to do with either Adventism or Christianity. However, he was known for his honest dealing in his career as a mechanic and as the owner of gas stations and used car lots in the Los Angeles area.[*]

One of Miles's favorite children, Dorothy (1908–2008) could do no wrong in his eyes—except for refusing to marry when he wanted her to. Years after his death, she became the wife of two highly influential Adventist evangelists in succession: Walter Priebe and, after Walter's death in 1950, Wilbur Dunn, who had at one time led the Seventh-day Adventist Church in present-day Sri Lanka. The longest-lived of the already long-lived "Kellogg tribe," Dorothy survived all of her siblings and lived to the age of one hundred.

Miles Justus (1910–2002), the teenaged co-builder of the Encinitas Boathouses, became a professional builder and contractor like his father and Murl. When his father retired in the early 1930s, he continued working in San Diego County until 1940. During this time, he erected some of the original hothouses for Paul Ecke's world-famous poinsettias, worked on the racetrack at Del Mar and worked for Douglas Fairbanks in Rancho Santa Fe.[†] A pacifist, Miles Justus fulfilled his military obligations during the Second World War by working in agriculture in Arkansas with the help of his wife, Ruth (née Howell). After the war, he supervised, virtually singlehandedly, the construction of the Adventists' Sunnydale Academy in Missouri from a disused army barracks. Even today, over half a century later, Sunnydale's original administration building and gymnasium continue to stand the test of time, just like the Boathouses, and are used by the campus's current population.[‡]

---

[*] Lloyd led an extremely colorful life as a young man. Among other things, he worked at San Diego's glamorous Hotel del Coronado and ran his own business shuttling sailors across the border into Mexico for liquor during Prohibition.

[†] One day, while working on a hotel in Rancho Santa Fe, Miles Justus saw a big man walk in with a beautiful blond woman on his arm. Miles Justus thought the man was Mexican and asked Anderson who he was. The response: "That's Douglas Fairbanks!" The lovely woman was Fairbanks's then-wife, Mary Pickford.

[‡] The full history of Sunnydale's construction is chronicled in the book *Born in a Barn*, published in 2009 by Miles Justus's two children, Dorothy Kellogg Rice and Miles J. Kellogg Jr.

THE KELLOGG FAMILY MEMBERS

The Parents

Miles Minor Kellogg: June 8, 1870–December 28, 1933
Ruth Jane Wood: March 7, 1871–August 30, 1962
Married June 8, 1891

And Their Children

Chester Everett: June 27, 1892–November 19, 1984
Irma Leona: July 3, 1895–March 4, 1989
Edith Viola: November 22, 1896–December 27, 1995
Walter Lewis: January 11, 1899–August 3, 1899
Vera Lorene: July 15, 1900–July 8, 1997
Francis Murl: February 1, 1902–February 3, 1994
Helen Pearl: March 9, 1903–August 19, 1963
Lloyd Galen: June 24, 1905–January 20, 1997
Dorothy Mae: January 25, 1908–September 10, 2008
Miles Justus: May 18, 1910–January 25, 2002

NOTES

Chapter 1

1. Chester Everett Kellogg, "Attempts at an Autobiography," 9.
2. Ruth Jane Wood Kellogg, "To My Children," 5.
3. M.P. Kellogg to Chester Everett Kellogg, unpublished letter, November 3, 1934, 2–5,.
4. Chester Kellogg, "Attempts at an Autobiography," 9.
5. "Mortuary," *Weekly Palladium*.

Chapter 2

6. Ruth Kellogg, "To My Children," 3.
7. Ibid., 1.
8. Ibid., 3.
9. Ibid., 1–2.
10. Ibid., 2.
11. Ibid., 3.

Chapter 3

12. "Mortuary." *Weekly Palladium*.

13. Ruth Kellogg, "To My Children," 3–4.
14. Ibid.
15. Ibid., 4.
16. "State Items," *Detroit Free Press*.
17. "Sodus," *Weekly Palladium*, November 4, 1892.
18. Ruth Kellogg, "To My Children," 5.
19. Ibid.

Chapter 4

20. Ibid.
21. "Sodus," *Weekly Palladium*, September 14, 1894.
22. "Kellogg Family, Former Residents," June 20, 1952.
23. Ibid.
24. Ruth Kellogg, "To My Children," 5.
25. Ibid., 6.
26. Ibid.
27. Ibid.
28. Ibid.
29. Chester Kellogg, "Attempts at an Autobiography," 3–10.
30. Edith Kellogg Tyrrel, interview by Betty McWhinny Aldrich.
31. Ruth Kellogg, "To My Children," 6.
32. Edith Kellogg Tyrrel to Sylvia Aldrich, unpublished letter.
33. Chester Everett Kellogg, obituary for Miles Minor Kellogg.
34. Chester Everett Kellogg, conversation with Betty McWhinny Aldrich.
35. Chester Kellogg, "Attempts at an Autobiography," 5.
36. Betty McWhinny Aldrich, personal genealogical notes.
37. Ibid.
38. Chester Kellogg, "Attempts at an Autobiography," 9–10

Chapter 5

39. Ibid., 3.
40. Ibid., 7–8.
41. Betty Aldrich, "Edith Tyrrel," 7.
42. Ibid., 6.
43. Ibid., 7.

44. Chester Kellogg, "Attempts at an Autobiography," 8.
45. Tyrrel, interview by Aldrich.
46. Chester Kellogg, "Attempts at an Autobiography," 8–9.
47. Ibid.

Chapter 6

48. Ibid., 11.
49. Ibid.
50. Aldrich, "Edith Tyrrel," 7.
51. Chester Kellogg, "Attempts at an Autobiography," 11.
52. Aldrich, "Edith Tyrrel," 8.
53. Homestead Entry Final Proof, Testimony of Claimant.
54. Chester and Clara Kellogg to Edith Tyrrel and Vera Hocking, unpublished letter.
55. Aldrich, "Edith Tyrrel," 2.
56. Chester Kellogg, " Attempts at an Autobiography," 11–13.
57. Ibid., 17.
58. Ibid., 13.
59. Ruth Kellogg, "To My Children," 6.
60. Ibid.
61. Chester Kellogg to Edith Tyrrel, unpublished letter.
62. Chester Kellogg, "Attempts at an Autobiography," 13.
63. U.S. Census 1880.
64. Homestead Entry Final Proof, Testimony of Claimant.

Chapter 7

65. Vera Kellogg Hocking, conversation with Betty Aldrich, unpublished notes.
66. Aldrich, "Edith Tyrrel," 8.
67. "Child's Reason," *Jackson Daily News*.
68. Vera Hocking, conversation with Betty Aldrich.
69. Aldrich, "Edith Tyrrel," 8–9.
70. Chester Kellogg, "Autobiography," 16–17.

Chapter 8

71. Homestead Entry Final Proof, Testimony of Claimant.
72. Ibid.
73. Ibid.
74. Homestead Entry Final Proof, Testimony of Witness.
75. Ibid.
76. Chester Kellogg, "Attempts at an Autobiography," 18.
77. Ibid.
78. Ibid., 18–19.
79. Ibid., 19.
80. Ibid., 14.
81. Ibid., 20.

Chapter 9

82. "Building Is Active around Encinitas," *Blade Tribune*.
83. "Encinitas Etchings," *Blade Tribune*, August 25, 1917.
84. Miles Justus Kellogg, oral history, unpublished audio recording.
85. "Encinitas Etchings," *Blade Tribune*, September 21, 1918.
86. Miles Minor Kellogg, handwritten paper.
87. "Encinitas Boy," *Blade Tribune*.
88. "Encinitas Etchings," *Blade Tribune*, September 21, 1918.

Chapter 10

89. "Encinitas," *Blade Tribune*, September 20, 1919.
90. "Encinitas," *Blade Tribune*, September 9, 1922.
91. *Coast-Dispatch*, February 12, 1925.
92. *Blade Tribune*, January 8, 1925.
93. *Coast-Dispatch*, February 12, 1925.
94. "Bonsall Briefs," *Blade Tribune*.
95. "Encinitas," *Blade Tribune*, January 24, 1920.
96. "Encinitas," *Blade Tribune*, August 20, 1921.
97. "Encinitas Etchings," *Blade Tribune*, September 15, 1917.
98. "Encinitas," *Blade Tribune*, June 28, 1919.
99. "Encinitas," *Blade Tribune*, January 24, 1920.

100. "Solana Beach," *Blade Tribune*.

101. Chester Kellogg, conversation with Betty Aldrich.

102. "Encinitas," *Blade Tribune*, May 22, 1924.

103. *Blade Tribune*, August 14, 1924.

Chapter 11

104. Miles Minor Kellogg to his family, unpublished letter from Boulder, Colorado.

105. Miles Minor Kellogg to his family, unpublished letter from Sodus, Berrien County, Michigan.

106. "Kellogg Returns from Eastern Trip," *Coast-Dispatch*.

107. "Old Bath House Wrecked," *Coast-Dispatch*.

108. *Coast-Dispatch*, October 25, 1929.

109. Miles Justus Kellogg, oral history.

110. Kellogg Rice and Zytkoskee, eds., *Born in a Barn*, 35.

111. Miles Justus Kellogg, oral history.

112. Miles Minor Kellogg, "To the People."

Chapter 12

113. Miles Minor Kellogg, arguments in support of the scriptural Sabbath.

114. "Real Estate," *Coast-Dispatch*.

115. Miles Minor Kellogg, "Progress of the Pilgrim Time."

116. *Coast-Dispatch*, October 25, 1929.

117. "Haven for Faithful," *San Diego Union and Daily Bee*.

118. Miles Minor Kellogg to Unknown Person (unpublished, circa 1931), author's collection.

119. Miles Minor Kellogg, "To the People."

120. "Spell of the Sea," *San Diego Union Tribune*.

121. "Olympia's Modern Noah," *San Francisco Examiner*.

122. Ibid.

123. "He's All Ready," *Santa Ynez Valley News*.

124. Miles Minor Kellogg to Theo Ward, unpublished draft.

Chapter 13

125. Chester Kellogg, conversation with Betty Aldrich.
126. "Rupe Moves," *Coast-Dispatch.*
127. Ibid.
128. "Rupe Building Sold," *Coast-Dispatch.*
129. Francis Murl Kellogg, conversation with Betty Aldrich, unpublished notes.
130. Miles Kellogg to his wife and children, unpublished letter from Glendale, California.
131. Butler to M.M. Kellogg.
132. Miles Minor Kellogg to Forest McWhinny.

Chapter 14

133. Betty Aldrich, memoirs written in preparation for interview, 1.
134. Tyrrel, interview by Aldrich.

Epilogue

135. Betty Aldrich, personal genealogical notes.
136. Chester E. Kellogg, obituary for Miles Minor Kellogg.
137. Edith Tyrrel to Sylvia Aldrich.
138. Mrs. Ethel W. White to the Honorable Richard M. Nixon.
139. Betty Aldrich, personal genealogical notes.
140. "In Loving Memory of Ruth J. Kellogg," *In Remembrance.*
141. Ibid.
142. Ruth Kellogg, "To My Children," 7.

BIBLIOGRAPHY

Aldrich, Betty McWhinny. Diary of trip to Wyoming and Boulder. Unpublished manuscript, n.d. Author's collection.

———. "Edith Tyrrel." Unpublished manuscript, n.d. Author's collection.

———. "Grandma Tyrrel's Memories with Jonathan Aldrich." Unpublished video recording, Christmas 1989/New Year's 1990. Author's collection.

———. "Melenda." Unpublished biographical sketch, n.d. Author's collection.

———. Memoirs written in preparation for interview by *Lifestyles*. Unpublished manuscript, n.d. Author's collection.

———. "Miles & Ruth." Unpublished manuscript, 1993. Author's collection.

———. Personal genealogical notes. Unpublished notes, n.d. Author's collection.

——— to Rochelle and Wynn Smith. Unpublished letter, n.d. Author's collection.

——— to Sylvia Aldrich. Unpublished letter, February 29, 1992. Author's collection.

Blade Tribune (Oceanside, CA), August 14, 1924. California Digital Newspaper Collection, University of California–Riverside Center for Bibliographical Studies and Research. https://cdnc.ucr.edu. (Hereafter cited as CDNC, UC–Riverside.)

———. "Bonsall Briefs." September 30, 1916. CDNC, UC–Riverside.

———. "Building Is Active around Encinitas." September 2, 1916. CDNC, UC–Riverside.

———, January 8, 1925. CDNC, UC–Riverside.

———. "Encinitas." August 20, 1921. CDNC, UC–Riverside.

———. "Encinitas." January 24, 1920. CDNC, UC–Riverside.

———. "Encinitas." June 28, 1919. CDNC, UC–Riverside.

———. "Encinitas." May 22, 1924. CDNC, UC–Riverside.

———. "Encinitas." November 18, 1922. CDNC, UC–Riverside.

———. "Encinitas." October 2, 1920. CDNC, UC–Riverside.

———. "Encinitas." September 9, 1922. CDNC, UC–Riverside.

———. "Encinitas." September 20, 1919. CDNC, UC–Riverside.

———. "Encinitas Boy Is Killed in France." August 31, 1918. CDNC, UC–Riverside.

———. "Encinitas Etchings." August 25, 1917. CDNC, UC–Riverside.

———. "Encinitas Etchings." September 15, 1917. CDNC, UC–Riverside.

———. "Encinitas Etchings." September 21, 1918. CDNC, UC–Riverside.

———. "Solana Beach a Busy Center." March 13, 1934. CDNC, UC–Riverside.

Butler, John Lowell to M.M. Kellogg. Unpublished letter, March 23, 1933. Author's collection.

Coast-Dispatch (Encinitas, CA). "Kellogg Returns from Eastern Trip." August 14, 1925. Microfilm.

———. "Old Bath House Wrecked." October 19, 1928. Microfilm.

———. "Pioneer Days Boom Told by Geo. Thebo." July 31, 1925. Microfilm.

———. "Real Estate." March 27, 1925. Microfilm.

———. "Rupe Building Sold." July 31, 1930. Microfilm.

———. "Rupe Moves into His New Building." June 8, 1928. Microfilm.

Detroit Free Press. "State Items." March 5, 1894. https://newspapers.com.

Dunn, Dorothy Kellogg. Conversation with Betty Aldrich. Unpublished notes, 1992. Author's collection.

——— to her brothers and sisters, nieces and nephews. Unpublished letter, December 17, 1964. Author's collection.

——— to Lloyd and Margaret Kellogg. Photocopy of unpublished letter, November 9, 1989. Author's collection.

Hocking, Vera Kellogg. Conversation with Betty McWhinny Aldrich. Unpublished notes, n.d. Author's collection.

———. "Life History Questionnaire." Unpublished manuscript, n.d. Author's collection.

——— to physician. Unpublished letter, n.d. Author's collection.

Homestead Entry Final Proof, Testimony of Claimant (Miles M. Kellogg), March 25, 1913. U.S. Land Office, Cheyenne, Wyoming, No. 03150, serial patent file No. 350516. National Archives, Record Group No. 49.

Homestead Entry Final Proof, Testimony of Witness (John Hobbs), March 25, 1913. U.S. Land Office, Cheyenne, Wyoming, No. 03150, serial patent file No. 350516. National Archives, Record Group No. 49.

"In Loving Memory of Ruth J. Kellogg." From *In Remembrance*. Placerville, CA: Memory Chapel, Inc.

Jackson Daily News (Jackson, MS). "The Child's Reason." December 15, 1906. https://newspapers.com.

Kellogg, Chester Everett and Clara, to Edith Kellogg Tyrrel and Vera Kellogg Hocking. Unpublished letter, n.d. Author's collection.

Kellogg, Chester Everett. "Attempts at an Autobiography." Unpublished manuscript, circa 1981. Author's collection.

———. Conversation with Betty McWhinny Aldrich. Unpublished audio recording, n.d. Author's collection.

———. Conversation with Betty McWhinny Aldrich. Unpublished notes, n.d. Author's collection.

———. Obituary for Miles Minor Kellogg. Unknown periodical, n.d. Author's collection.

——— to Edith Kellogg Tyrrel. Unpublished letter, July 21, 1984. Author's collection.

Kellogg Family Bible.

"Kellogg Family, Former Residents, Visit in Boulder." June 20, 1952. Author's collection.

Kellogg, Francis Murl. Conversation with Betty McWhinny Aldrich. Unpublished notes, early 1990s. Author's collection.

Kellogg, Lloyd Galen. Conversation with Betty McWhinny Aldrich. Unpublished notes, December 13, 1992. Author's collection.

———. Oral history with Dorothy Kellogg Dunn. Unpublished audio recording, n.d. Author's collection.

Kellogg, Miles Justus. Conversation with Betty McWhinny Aldrich. Unpublished notes, August 29, 1993. Author's collection.

———. Conversation with Betty McWhinny Aldrich. Unpublished notes, July 1992. Author's collection.

———. Oral history. Unpublished audio recording, April 1992. Author's collection.

Kellogg, Miles Justus, and Vera Kellogg Hocking. Oral history with Betty McWhinny Aldrich. Unpublished notes, July 1992. Author's collection.

Kellogg, Miles Minor. Arguments in support of the scriptural Sabbath. Unpublished manuscript, n.d. Author's collection.

———. Handwritten paper. Unpublished manuscript, n.d. Author's collection.

———. "The Progress of the Pilgrim Time." Unpublished manuscript, n.d. Author's collection.

——— to Forest McWhinny from Brawley, California. Unpublished letter, June 4, 1931. Author's collection.

——— to his family from Denver, Colorado. Unpublished letter, June 28, 1925. Author's collection.

——— to his family from Sodus, Berrien County, Michigan. Unpublished letter, ca. July 1925. Author's collection.

——— to his wife and children. Unpublished letter, June 1, ca. 1932. Author's collection.

——— to Theo Ward. Unpublished draft of letter, May 19, 1931. Author's collection.

———. "To the People of This District." Unknown periodical. Author's collection.

Kellogg, M.P. to Chester Everett Kellogg. Unpublished letter, November 3, 1934. Author's collection.

Kellogg, Ruth Jane Wood to Mrs. W.W. Pogson. Unpublished postcard, n.d. Author's collection.

———. "To My Children." Unpublished manuscript, 1936/37. Author's collection.

Rice, Dorothy Kellogg, and Adrian Zytkoskee, eds. *Born in a Barn: Sunnydale Academy, the Early Years*. Self-published, Centralia, MI: Richman Graphic Services, June 2009.

San Diego Union Tribune. "Spell of the Sea." April 10, 1933. UCSD Geisel Library Collection, electronic archives.

———. "'Faithful' Fail to Buy Arks, So He'll Rent 'Em." April 5, 1931.

San Diego Union and Daily Bee. "Haven for Faithful." April 5, 1931. UCSD Geisel Library Collection, electronic archives.

San Francisco Examiner. "Olympia's Modern Noah and His Ark All Ready for the Next Flood." December 16, 1928. https://newspapers.com.

Santa Ynez Valley News (Solvang, CA). "He's All Ready with an Ark for Second Flood." August 28, 1931. https://newspapers.com.

St. Pierre, Evangeline McWhinny. Conversation with Nancy Aldrich Brupbacher. Unpublished notes, n.d. Author's collection.

Tonn-Oliver, Kathleen Priebe. Conversation with author. Unpublished notes, March 27, 2018. Author's collection.

Tyrrel, Edith Kellogg. Interview by Betty McWhinny Aldrich. Unpublished video recording, n.d. Author's collection.

———. Memorial service. Unpublished video recording, December 1995. Author's collection.

——— to Sylvia Aldrich. Unpublished letter, ca.1971. Author's collection.

U.S. Census 1850. https://www.familysearch.org/en/.

U.S. Census 1880. https://www.familysearch.org/en/.

Weekly Palladium (Benton Harbor, MI). "Hymeneal." June 12, 1891. https://newspapers.com.

———. "Mortuary." June 20, 1890. https://newspapers.com.

———. "Sodus." November 4, 1892. https://newspapers.com.

———. "Sodus." September 14, 1894. https://newspapers.com.

White, Mrs. Ethel W. to the Honorable Richard M. Nixon, Vice President of U.S.A. Photocopy of unpublished letter, September 26, 1960. Author's collection.

ABOUT THE AUTHOR

Rachel Brupbacher is a great-great-granddaughter of Miles Minor Kellogg. She holds degrees in French, German and history. In keeping with the Kellogg family's rich tradition of music making, she is also an accomplished, classically trained singer, violinist and violist.